Samuel
Bland
Arnold

Memoirs of a
Lincoln Conspirator

EDITED BY MICHAEL W. KAUFFMAN

HERITAGE BOOKS, INC.

Library of Congress Cataloging-in-Data

Arnold, Samuel Bland (1834-1906)
    Memoirs of a Lincoln Conspirator

Includes Index.

ISBN 0-7884-0367-2

1. Lincoln, Abraham -- assassination 2. Arnold, Samuel Bland

Published 1995 by

HERITAGE BOOKS, INC.
1540E Pointer Ridge Place
Bowie, Maryland 20716
1-800-398-7709

A Complete Catalog Listing Hundreds of Titles
On History, Genealogy, and Americana
Available Free Upon Request

Printed in the United States of America

Table of Contents

*Mr. Arnold Shunned Interviews---Claims "Innocent Con-
demned"---His Guilt Was But A Thought---Tells of Plots That
Failed---Story Recalled by a Death---Surratt in Canada---
"The Dry Tortugas a Hell"---A Fateful Letter to Booth---Gov-
ernment Suspicions Aroused---Johnson's Approval of
Sentence*

*Confederacy Exonerated---Booth Found in a Barn
Rebel Officials Blamed by Johnson*

*Gen. Hartranft's Plea for Reprieve---Hopes Dashed on Bay-
onets---The Final Failure to Obtain Clemency---Gen. Hancock Sees A Tearstained Face---Some Political After Effects
of the Execution*

*Arnold's Story Begins---Booth Had Large Income---Early
Preparations---A Mother's Dreams---The Parts Alotted---
Another Plan Hatched---Conspiracy Abandoned---Surratt in
Richmond---Arnold Placed Under Arrest*

*Arnold's Life---Before Meeting Booth---Dr. Mudd's Connec-
tion---No Reward for Deed---How the South Felt---Arnold
Not a Knight of the Golden Circle*

*Arnold's Background---War Changed Friendship---Left
Baltimore But to Return---A Fateful Journey to the City---
First Meeting With Booth---The Conspiracy Plans Outlined---
No Mercenary Incentive---Booth's Canadian Visit---Booth
Was a Monomaniac---Opportunities to Capture Lincoln Was-
ted---"Gas" Man Refused to Participate.*

*Idleness and Discontent---Plotters Spellbound by Booth---
Booth's Plan a Quixotic Undertaking---Actor Makes Still Another Appeal---Had Booth But Returned to Acting---Two Detectives Arrive at Fortress Monroe---Other Names Mentioned
by Detectives---Witnesses "Blinded by Gold"---Arnold Encoun-*

List of Illustrations

Acknowledgements

No worthwhile project could ever be completed without the help, advice, and encouragement of others. In this case, I owe a debt of gratitude to many friends and experts in the field. My thanks to Percy E. Martin, longtime authority on Samuel B. Arnold, who has willingly shared his research with me, and who has taken me to many of the sites connected with Arnold's life. His articles in the Baltimore County Historical Society's newsletter, *History Trails*, (Summer 1982 and Autumn 1990 through Spring 1991) are highly recommended. Thanks to Myra-Ann Rutledge for sharing her enthusiasm and her research, and to George L. Kackley, a great friend who has given me much information about the Arnold family genealogy.

Rev. Robert L. Keesler has generously provided me with a scrapbook containing original newspaper clippings of the Sam Arnold memoirs. Born in Arnold's own neighborhood of Waverly, Father Keesler has always taken a keen interest in the conspirators and in Maryland Confederate history. It was he who first located the photograph of William Arnold's house in Hookstown, and who made it available to me. Laurie Verge, site manager of the Surratt Tavern in Clinton, Maryland, has supplied me with many important contacts, and with much information on the Booth conspiracy. She has always been a great help in all my endeavors. Thanks, also, to the members of the Surratt Society for all their continued assistance and support.

At the National Archives, Michael Musick and William Lind were especially helpful. They, and the Central Search Room staff, have always given prompt and professional assistance whenever I needed it. Thanks as well to the staffs of the Maryland Historical Society, the Library of Congress (Manuscripts Division), and the Folger Shakespeare Library.

I would like to acknowledge the help and support of Lewis G. Schmidt, of Allentown, Pa., for sharing his tremendous knowledge of Fort Jefferson, and that of Candida Ewing Steel, of Annapolis, Md., for helping to locate some files relating to Dr. Mudd's escape attempt.

Eugene and Dennis Doyle were very generous with their information on their ancestor, Oreon Mann Jackson (Sam Arnold's sister). Special thanks to them for the pictures of George and Mary Jane Arnold. Carl and Joan Miles kindly allowed me to visit and photograph their home, in which Sam Arnold once lived.

My efforts have always benefitted from the friendship and guidance of John C. Brennan. His knowledge and enthusiasm for the subject have made him the dean of "Booth buffs". I thank him for many years of unfailing assistance.

Steve Miller has been very generous with his time and his computer. I thank him for the photo reproductions, and for all the times he has come through for me. Thanks to Ivy Jane (Mrs. Stephen Z.) Starr for granting permission to publish her late husband's photo of Col. Grenfell.

Finally, thanks to my wife, Mary, and our daughter, Emily, who have surrendered all their claims on my spare time, so I would be free to work on this book. Without their understanding, none of this would be possible.

Michael W. Kauffman
Calvert County, Maryland
August, 1995

Introduction

Sometimes a person's fate can turn on what seems to be an insignificant event. For Samuel Bland Arnold, that event was a missed meeting with an old friend.

On the night of April 14, 1865, the world was stunned by the news of Abraham Lincoln's assassination. Lincoln had been shot from behind as he watched a play at Ford's Theatre in Washington. At about the same time, Secretary of State William Seward was savagely attacked in his sickbed a few blocks away. Rumors of a far-reaching conspiracy sent a frenzied panic all across the North.

It was obvious that the assassin, actor John Wilkes Booth, had conspired with others. But how large was the conspiracy? And whom would they attack next? More importantly, where had the conspirators come from, and where did they disappear? Booth's desperate act left a flood of questions urgently in need of answers.

Evidence rushed in from every direction, and much of it seemed to point northeast, toward Baltimore. The name of Booth had long been associated with the Monumental City, and Lincoln's killer was quite well known there. John Wilkes Booth had spent his childhood in the city's Old Town area and at the family farm, Tudor Hall, near Bel Air. A great many local people counted themselves among his friends, and these included influential citizens both in and out of his own theatrical profession.

Baltimore had been a strongly pro-Southern place, and throughout the war Lincoln had kept the city in line with a sometimes heavy-handed military presence. His declaration of martial law there gave rise to an intricate web of subversives devoted to thwarting the administration at every turn. Suppressing their efforts had been an enormous task, but now an even greater job lay ahead for the man charged with that responsibility, Provost Marshal James L. McPhail.

Throughout the night of the assassination, McPhail gathered his men, consulted with military officials, and set about looking into Booth's local connections. It wouldn't take long to find out that one of McPhail's own acquaintences, Mike O'Laughlen, had been close to the assassin. That would be worth a close look, but as this and other leads came in, a more urgent message arrived by telegraph from Washington. The provost marshal there, Col. Timothy Ingraham, had sent a squad of officers on a midnight raid of Booth's hotel room. In the assassin's trunk they found a letter, written to Booth a few weeks earlier by a Baltimore County man who signed himself "Sam". This note referred to an unspecified scheme involving Booth, but which "Sam" had since abandoned. The writer warned that detectives and suspicious relatives were watching him closely, and advised Booth to wait for a "more propitious" time to act. Then "Sam" dropped an astounding comment: "I would prefer your first query," he wrote, "go and see how it will be taken at R------d,' and ere long I shall be better prepared to again be with you."

The War Department had gathered a wealth of evidence on the Lincoln conspiracy, but hardly anything could match the value and importance of the "Sam" letter. This was proof of a conspiracy, but it was even more. Here, on four handwritten pages, was unmistakable proof that the assassin of President Lincoln had intended to seek Confederate approval for his crime. This was explosive news, and it seemed to come from good authority.

It became McPhail's job to find out who had written the letter, and for this he sought his clues in the text itself. Obviously, the author was an articulate man and a knowledge-able insider. He and Booth had once been intimate, but a coolness had developed between them, and lately "Sam" was getting angry at his old friend. His break from the plot had put him in a real bind; past association made him guilty, but he had done nothing overt, and might even consider himself innocent. Thus, his current status made him a better informant than defendant, and detectives might use that leverage to gain information from him on the promise of freedom. But all that would come later. For now, just finding him was a top priority of the government.

"Sam" had dated his letter from Hookstown, a tiny hamlet along the Hookstown Pike (now the Reisterstown Road) near Baltimore. The area was mostly farmland, and one tract there was owned by William S. Arnold. Everyone in the neigh-borhood knew that Arnold had a brother named Sam, who often came up from the city to stay there. Sam Arnold was a former Confederate soldier and, as it developed, a good friend of John Wilkes Booth.

McPhail's men searched the Arnold place and the adjoining farm of Sam's uncle, William J. Bland. The suspect himself was long gone, having taken a clerk's position at Fortress Monroe, Virginia, two weeks before. It was there, on the afternoon of April 17th, that detectives caught up with

Samuel B. Arnold and placed him under arrest for conspiracy to kill the president.

Returning to Baltimore, Arnold confessed that he had taken part in a conspiracy, but he insisted their plan was only to capture President Lincoln, and not to kill him. Their purpose, he said, was to ransom the president for prisoners of war.

From the first, Sam Arnold acknowledged his authorship of the suspicious letter. He explained that he had written it after failing to meet Booth one day at Barnum's Hotel. The latter had summoned him there on urgent business, but then left without allowing him time to get there. While Arnold had always preferred to deal with his friend face-to-face, on this occasion Booth gave him no choice.

The Barnum's Hotel meeting was never supposed to happen. Booth's summons was just his way of making sure that this recently departed conspirator could report nothing to the government without proving his own guilt in the process. That incriminating letter (and Booth's subsequent reminder to Arnold that he had retained it) was an insurance policy. Had Arnold actually met Booth at Barnum's, there would have been no letter, no paper trail, and no reason for history to remember Samuel Bland Arnold.

The assassination of Abraham Lincoln was avenged by the killing of Booth on April 26th by a New York cavalry detachment. Though Sam Arnold denied any involvement in a murder plot, he and seven others stood trial a few weeks later before a military commission in Washington. Taking their cue from the "Sam letter", prosecutors tried to build a case against Confederate leaders as well, but in this they failed. After sitting impassively through the seven-week trial, all eight defendants were found guilty of the charges. That surprised noone. Many believed it couldn't have happened any other way.

For drama, intrigue, and historical importance, the Lincoln assassination has few parallels. The American public developed a boundless fascination for all the details of the conspiracy and for those who took part in it. But despite the investigation and all the coverage it received, many issues remained unresolved. Souvenir hunters had run off with evidence, and careless questioning left many points unsettled. Lack of coordination, among other things, had hampered the investigation and left the case full of holes. Perhaps detectives had done well by the standards of their own day, but a century later we have grown used to something a great deal more complete.

Pre-trial investigations yielded only trivia and gossip about the accused. Detectives learned, for example, that George Atzerodt suffered from consumption; that David Herold's mother always locked him out of the house if he didn't come home by ten o'clock; and that Mike O'Laughlen once studied the art of ornamental plastering. These were humanizing facts, of no use to the prosecution or the press.[1]

Of Sam Arnold, the evidence was sparse and contradictory. A man named John Broom described him as a good scholar, and rather passive in nature. Robert Mowry, on the other hand, called Arnold a hard-fighting, aggressive man. Mowry also told detectives that the suspect had a habit of checking into Baltimore hotels with women who only pretended to be his wife. An undated War Department memo, intended as a biographical "sketch" for the prosecution, was hardly damaging to his case. The memo noted his fine education and high social connections. Arnold's fatal flaw, it said, was his inclination toward "bad associations." This was hardly incriminating.[2]

The Lincoln conspiracy trial was not intended as a fact-finding procedure, and it did little to flesh out the public's knowledge of the plot. In fact, both sides had a strong interest in keeping information off the record. This was especially true in Sam Arnold's case. The defense naturally wanted to avoid any discussion of Arnold's part in the conspiracy. Attorney Thomas Ewing, Jr., focused instead on testimony that the defendant had not seen Booth for almost a month before the crime was committed. Arnold's brothers, William and Frank, testified that Sam had been staying in Hookstown for the last part of March. Minnie Poole and Jacob Smith verified this. John Wharton, Charles Hall, and George Craig testified that Arnold had been in Fortress Monroe since April 2nd. On this alone the defense rested.[3]

On the other side, Assistant Judge Advocate John A. Bingham based his argument primarily on legal reasoning, rather than on the facts of the case. Bingham wanted to prove only that Arnold was an intimate friend of Booth, and that he did indeed write the "Sam" letter. To that end, witnesses testified that Arnold was often seen in Booth's company and that he had received messages and letters from the assassin, sometimes with money enclosed. This, in Bingham's view, proved a criminal connection.

The prosecution built its case on these sketchy facts. But testimony told only part of the story. So many details of the plot were known only to those charged in the trial, and the law allowed them to keep their silence. Without their testimony, the whole story could never be known.

If Judge Advocate Bingham had one golden moment in the trial, it was undoubtedly the tactical victory he scored in arguing the case against Sam Arnold. Bingham brought up the fact that Arnold had once joined the Confederate Army. This, he argued, was in itself a criminal act -- an attempt to overthrow the United States Government. The killing of the president had the same objective, and therefore, Arnold's war record was proof of his intent to further the conspiracy. It made no difference whether or not he was present when John Wilkes Booth carried his own plan into effect. Arnold was still guilty.

Bingham's reasoning made a conspirator of every man who had ever served in the Southern armies. His argument opened the door to prosecutions of Jefferson Davis and other high-ranking Confederates who had actually been named with Arnold as co-defendants, but who were still at large when the indictments were handed down. Over Ewing's objections, Bingham vigorously argued that point, and the military commission agreed. The defense was effectively silenced on a vital point.

The Lincoln conspiracy trial lasted from May 9th through June 30th. Seven defendants were found guilty of conspiring to kill the president, but the eighth (Edman Spangler) was convicted only of assisting the assassin in his escape.

Within hours after the verdicts were announced, four of the prisoners were taken into the penitentiary yard and hanged. Sam Arnold was more fortunate. Sentenced to life at hard labor, he joined the three remaining "state prisoners", and was shipped off to serve his sentence in the Dry Tortugas, a small chain of islands in the Gulf of Mexico.

With its principal players dead and others in seclusion, the Lincoln conspiracy might have become one of history's great mysteries. The investigative process had run its course, and all records were sealed and locked away.

From the earliest days, public attention was focused on the controversies surrounding the case: the questionable legality of the military trial, the evidence prosecutors had failed to bring forth, and especially, the hanging of Mary Surratt -- a woman who, according to popular opinion, might have been innocent after all. There was no discussion of Booth's motives, or of the political mileu in which the conspiracy had developed. The fires of the war still smoldered, and proper decorum demanded that the killing be condemned without further comment. John T. Ford, however, broke that tradition in an 1878 newspaper interview. Ford, who had known the assassin well, described Booth as a human being with a rational, though misguided, sense of duty.[4]

Gradually others came forward to offer their insights but, in general, interest and memories had waned. The most knowledgeable sources were unable or unwilling to speak out.

Booth himself died on the run, leaving only a few dramatic ramblings. Those charged with conspiracy kept relatively quiet, even after the legal process had run its course. John H. Surratt was the exception, but only briefly. Soon after a deadlocked jury set him free, Surratt started on a lecture tour. He had given only a few speeches before federal agents arrested him for non-payment of taxes. Surratt lowered his public profile,[5] and with rare exceptions, he remained quiet for the rest of his life. His lecture was the only inside account of the Lincoln conspiracy -- that is, until Sam Arnold was moved to write this memoir.

We are fortunate it was Sam Arnold, of all the defendants, who committed his memories to paper. Like David Herold and Dr. Mudd, he was an educated man (all three were alumni of Georgetown College). Like Ned Spangler and Mike O'Laughlen, he was a close friend of Booth. Like Lewis Powell and John Surratt, he was a trusted member of the inner circle. So while each participant in the scheme might have brought an important perspective to the story, Sam Arnold had an advantage from nearly every angle. This was true even in the Dry Tortugas, where his job in the provost marshal's office gave him access to prison records. Making use of the opportunity, Arnold took copious notes on everything that came within his observation.

Sam Arnold went into seclusion after he was pardoned in 1869, and he seldom spoke of the plot, even to his friends. But the popular version of Booth's conspiracy was inaccurate, and it gnawed at him for years. In the early 1890s Arnold made up his mind to set the record straight on all the "lies" and "slanders" he had seen in print. So he wrote down his own views, prompted by the notes and diaries he had kept while in custody. Adding his own research on events he had not personally witnessed, he produced a first-rate memoir that was fresh, interesting, and astonishingly accurate, given the passage of time.

When editors at the *Baltimore American* learned that Arnold was working on a manuscript, they contacted him about its publication. Arnold insisted that anything he wrote could only be printed after his death. But a strange occurrence persuaded him to change his mind. In October, 1902, another man named Sam Arnold died, and some newspapers mistakenly reported that the famous conspirator had passed away. They ran obituaries on the wrong man, and in the process, gave Arnold a chance to see how his own death might be reported. He was not pleased.

Editors corrected their mistake, but in the meantime, they had reawakened interest in Sam Arnold's story. The

American sent Edward Lollman to visit Arnold on his farm, and Lollman found the old man friendly and eager to talk. They struck a deal. The paper printed Arnold's story in serial form, while syndicating it to other newspapers throughout the country.

In "Lincoln Conspiracy and the Conspirators", Sam Arnold gave us the most complete and insightful look at the Booth conspiracy and how it operated. He reported the assassin's moods, his words and his motivations from the earliest days of the kidnap conspiracy. He showed us how Booth recruited people into the plot, and how he kept them from betraying their secrets to the authorities. And he reported some events to which he was the only surviving witness, such as that first conspiratorial meeting in Barnum's in 1864. If not for Sam Arnold's account, these events might have been lost to history.

The story was remarkable, but far from perfect. Sam Arnold had a limited role in a compartmentalized plot. He was never privy to all its machinations, and neither was anyone else. Unlike Lewis Powell and John Surratt, he did not travel extensively on Booth's behalf, though he remained near the action throughout. He never knew the names of all the other conspirators, and he probably did not maintain ties to the Confederate government. Clearly, Arnold was excluded from some of the plot's inner workings. But he knew a great deal about what happened, and for that reason his work is a vital source. Unfortunately, though, he sidestepped some important issues.

He did not, for example, explain the text of his March 27th letter. What did he mean when he referred to Booth's query to "see how it will be taken in R------d"? He stated flatly that high Confederate officials were not involved in the murder, but he declined to discuss the matter to any great extent. Moreover, his writings were full of puzzling gaps. They set forth a detailed description of life in prison, but they hardly contain a word about his fellow conspirators who shared a miserable existence there. The most striking omission is the absence of any comment on the case of his cellmate, Michael O'Laughlen. Arnold ignores him so completely that in telling about the end of the yellow fever epidemic, Arnold writes that "happily, we lived through it all," when in fact, O'Laughlen had died from the disease.

Arnold's memoirs came at an active period in Lincoln assassination studies. They followed soon after the publication of Osborn H. Oldroyd's *The Assassination of Abraham Lincoln* (1901), a straightforward narrative of the conspiracy and its aftermath. Both accounts were non-sensationalist, but they appeared at a time when the trend was quite the opposite. During the preceding decade, General Thomas M. Harris, a member of the military commission that tried Arnold, published *The Assassination of Lincoln* (1892), in which he claimed that the Pope had ordered Lincoln's killing. This theme was nothing new, but it found resonance again in the nativist and anti-Catholic movements to which, ironically, Booth himself had once belonged. Harris's work was followed by the controversial book *The Judicial Murder of Mary Surratt* (1895), in which David M. DeWitt argued that the Lincoln conspiracy trial was illegal, and that Mrs. Surratt was unjustly convicted and "murdered" in a government "reign of terror."

Sam Arnold was quite sympathetic to DeWitt's theme of a corrupt and heartless government. But the idea took a new twist with the next major publication to follow the Arnold memoirs. In *The Escape and Suicide of John Wilkes Booth* (1907) Finis L. Bates told of a massive government coverup of John Wilkes Booth's successful escape from justice. Bates claimed that the assassin lived for many years after the president's death, and the War Department hid the fact that its soldiers had killed the wrong man in Booth's place.

Surrounded by these sensationalist books and theories, Samuel Bland Arnold's reminiscences attracted relatively little notice at the time of their appearance. Later, they were completely overshadowed by the works of an Austrian-born chemist named Otto Eisenschiml. Like DeWitt and Bates, Eisenschiml invoked the demons of governmental coverup, but his first book, *Why Was Lincoln Murdered?* (1937) carried that idea to the extreme. Eisenschiml charged Secretary of War Edwin Stanton with instigating the president's murder, allowing the assassin to escape, and then putting innocent victims on trial in mock retribution for his own crimes.

Clearly, Otto Eisenschiml and Sam Arnold shared an unrestrained hostility for Edwin Stanton. For Sam Arnold, who had borne the full weight of War Department tyranny, this was a deeply personal matter, and he never pulled his punches when writing of the detested War Secretary. For that reason, we may be certain that if he had even suspected a Stanton connection to the plot, he would have reported it with glee. However, it seems he never even conceived of such a bizarre idea.

"Lincoln Conspiracy and the Conspirators" made its first appearance in serial form during the month of December, 1902. By arrangement with the *Baltimore American*, a number of major newspapers carried the series through its full run of two weeks. A few editors, however, were incensed by Arnold's charges of torture at the hands of United States soldiers, and they cancelled the last installments. One wrote that he had no room in his columns for the complaints of traitors; Sam Arnold had only gotten what he deserved. Thirty-seven years after the fact, Lincoln's assassination still had the power to stir the emotions.

In 1943, a prominent antiquarian book dealer named Charles F. Heartman published Arnold's original manuscript in book form. The volume, entitled *Defence and Prison Experiences of a Lincoln Conspirator,* was printed without notes, index, or corrected spellings. It is an accurate transcript of Arnold's own writing, but its run was limited to 199 copies, and it is extremely hard to find.

This volume reproduces the 1902 newspaper version. The text, headlines, subheads, and chapter breaks are preserved here exactly as in the original. However, there are exceptions: obvious typographical errors that appeared in the newspaper are corrected here. New chapter titles are used here from Chapter Four on, while the newspaper version kept the same title every day. The reader will note that Sam Arnold is sometimes referred to in the third person, and sometimes in the first person. This is because the newspapers included commentary by an editor of the *American*, who wrote three introductory chapters, and who often failed to make the distinction between his own writing and that of Mr. Arnold. These narrative splices were sometimes subtle, though not always. They proved impossible to identify with any degree of finesse.

The actor John Barrymore once said that reading footnotes was like running downstairs every few minutes on one's wedding night to answer the doorbell. While the sentiment is duly noted, so is the necessity for an occasional intrusion. There was much in the Arnold narrative that seemed to require clarification. In particular, the names of soldiers and guards were left out of the 1902 publication, evidently at the editors' insistence. Every name that appeared in the original manuscript has been restored here in the notes. To keep the record straight, each story or accusation has been checked against the official records for verification, where possible.

Proper names within the text are left in their original form, although Arnold often erred in the spellings -- particularly in the case of soldiers at Fort Jefferson. In both the notes and the index, all names are given in the form used by the subjects themselves, as indicated by the best evidence. Michael O'-Laughlen's surname, for example, is almost always spelled with an "-in" ending, though the O'Laughlen family spelled it with an "-en". Lacking direct evidence, name spellings appear as they did on government records.

Finally, three appendices are included to supplement the Arnold text. Appendix A is a verbatim transcript of the statement Arnold gave to Marshal McPhail soon after his arrest. It shows the conspirator's earliest explanation of the plot, given before research and long years of contemplation could possibly have intruded upon his memory. The statement is included here to illustrate the remarkable consistency of Arnold's public words on the subject.

Appendix B is a letter that Arnold wrote to his terminally ill mother just after the close of the conspiracy trial, and before he had learned of his own sentence. Penned in a cramped, dark prison cell, the letter gives some idea of the anguish Arnold felt at one of the lowest moments of his life. It is a surprisingly eloquent statement of despair by a man who was held up to the world as a shiftless, ignorant thug.

To complete the record, Arnold's lengthy obituary from the *Baltimore American* is added as Appendix C.

An index, notes, and appendices are included in the interest of making this volume the most complete and reliable version of the Arnold memoirs available. Taken as a whole, *Memoirs of a Lincoln Conspirator* should be a worthwhile addition to the Lincoln assassination literature, with much information that has not been available to the public thus far.

Chapter One

ARNOLD'S STORY
of
LINCOLN CONSPIRACY
—

One of the Famous Plotters Breaks the Silence of Years.

———

RECITAL OF SCHEMING AND TORTURE

———

How Booth, Arnold and Others Planned to Abduct the President

Graphic Description of Events Before and After the Assassination.

———

Mr. Arnold Shunned Interviews---Claims "Innocent Condemned"---His Guilt Was But A Thought---Tells of Plots That Failed---Story Recalled by a Death--- Surratt in Canada---"The Dry Tortugas a Hell"---A Fateful Letter to Booth--- Government Suspicions Aroused---Johnson's Approval of Sentence

[Sunday, December 7, 1902]

A most important and interesting document, dealing with the stirring events just preceding and subsequent to the assassination of President Abraham Lincoln, has come into the possession of *The American*, and will be presented to its readers in serial form. The author of the manuscript is Samuel Bland Arnold, one of the famous Lincoln conspirators who now, for the first time, at the age of 68, unseals the lips pledged to secrecy before the kidnapping plot was consummated, to tell all of the facts in the most minute detail of that history making epoch.

It is a wonderful story that this manuscript of Samuel B. Arnold unfolds -- a story of plots to capture the Chief Executive of the nation and convey him within the Confederate lines, conceived under the supposed impulses of patriotism to the South; of passions stirred to the depths of human souls as nothing but the impulses of hearts embittered by civil strife could engender, and of imprisonment, cruelty and torture.

Samuel B. Arnold, 1902

"It has not been written through malice or vindictiveness; I have confined myself to the truth," says Arnold, after a recitation of circumstances, which, in these days of internal peace, prosperity, and happiness, when the last traces of the bitterness of war have been swept aside forever, read like the revelation of some horrible nightmare, impossible of a reality.

An autobiographical recitation of wrongs by a man who can never forget, a man who seeks seclusion and avoids his fellow man, a misanthropist by his own statement. *The American* presents his life story upon his own basis; a public now unprejudiced and unbiased to sit in judgment upon its statements.

"The burnt child dreads the fire," writes Arnold, and in his misanthropic feelings, a hatred of mankind conceived and fostered in a contact with the stern arm of military law, he had intended to let his story slumber until he himself had passed into the great unknown, when he thought that conditions might be ripe for the reception of his recital.

In his own mind's eye, the cloud which had hung for well nigh 40 years had never been lightened or lessened, and it was not until recently that the conclusion was reached that his story could now be read and digested without passion, and each judge fairly as to its merits or demerits. With this determination established, Mr. Arnold consented to give his manuscript to the world through *The American*.

Shunned Interviews.

Only as late as October 17 last, Mr. Arnold was firm and determined not to give forth the manuscript for publication. On that date, in answer to a letter of a relative asking that he make the true story public in order that his side of the affair might stand against that of his prosecutors, Mr. Arnold wrote as follows:[1]

"I received yours of the 10th instant, and owing to indisposition could not answer until now. I have perused your letter carefully, and duly considered your propositions, and I see no reason why I should reopen an issue settled in the public mind now nearly 40 years. Justice is no part of the human race. To tear a man's character to pieces and to drag his name in the mire and filth is more eagerly sought after than to elevate him. The lie placed upon the pages of history can never be removed, nor would they even if Jesus Christ came to appear as a witness for you. Why, then, should I speak?

"I, who know nothing in regard to the affair, beyond the sufferings and inhuman punishment heaped upon me by the United States government, the tortures inflicted surpassing the inquisition in Spain, before even guilt or innocence had been established, though that lynch law commission convened not to mete out justice, but condemnation, to appease the public cry for vengeance. I have quietly borne my sufferings these 40 years, and propose doing so until the end, when, no doubt, I will be confronted with the members of the court and its prosecutors, when the guilt and innocence of both victim and court will be unraveled, and the truth established as to who were the authors direct of the subordination *[sic]* of the perjuries committed in our trial.

"Innocent Condemned."

"The man, the pigmy, under the prosecution of the law, gained the point, and condemned innocent persons to death and imprisonment -- they gratified their ambition and shed innocent blood without a shudder -- but before God's tribunal they will be made to answer and the murderers and assassins will be known. I will not permit anyone to interview me -- I would not verbally speak to any man upon the subject -- for a burnt child dreads the fire. When arrested I spoke but five words, which were reported just the reverse as spoken, the witness not looking to the innocence of the man, but desirous of proving guilt, to gain a portion of the huge reward offered for the apprehension and conviction. He even put in his claim, but through my father and Mr. Maulsby, his claim was turned down.[2]

"Under existing circumstances I shall forever keep my lips closed to interviewers, and, should I ever come before the public, it shall be in black and white, sworn to before a notary public. Of course I know nothing of the assassination plot. The kidnapping was of such a quixotic nature that there is nothing in it, and with the last no overt act was committed, therefore, no proceedings could be established under the law. I will cease to write of the harrowing subject, it but angers me."

Guilt But a Thought.

In a subsequent letter, consenting to the publication, Mr. Arnold says, in part:

"My guilt was but a thought; the government made it a crime. Thoughts exist in the minds of men, but remain dormant, never coming to the surface, never executed, hence to make such a crime, in my particular case, would make it criminal in the case of all. However, such a thing will not hold good in law. In my statement I deal with facts alone -- indisputable facts. They describe the horrible tortures inflicted before, during, and after trial, in fact condemned before any kind of evidence had been adduced before the court. It also describes the dreadful scenes witnessed during my incarceration at the Dry Tortugas, giving in detail those acts, besides the officers who perpetrated them.

"Neither malice nor prejudice prompts my action. No man in this land loves his country more than I do. None are more patriotic, none more just, honorable or truthful, possessing a heart of kindness and tenderness, equal to that of a woman. I can produce witnesses of the very best blood and standing in the state to vouch for my manhood. They have known me from my earliest boyhood, and can vouch for my purity of heart. Today in my old age I am by them respected and loved.

"The cloud which for nearly 40 years had hung over my

head prevented me from obtaining lucrative employment, besides it so shadowed my life that I had almost become a misanthropist. I was never better satisfied than in my own seclusion and retirement. My treatment had been of such a nature that I had no desire to mix with mankind. I had lost all confidence in the human race. Now going on 69 years of age, my health is shattered and crippled from rheumatism, contracted during my incarceration. I have passed the age to ever end employment to bridge over the short span between the present and my death.

Plots That Failed.

The manuscript of Arnold, in relation to its preparation, extends over a long period of years. That portion in which a most interesting account is given of the inception of the plots to kidnap President Lincoln, with their successive failures and the reasons therefor, giving names, dates and locations connected therewith, was written in the year 1867, while Arnold was confined in the Dry Tortugas, Florida, and attested to before a notary of the public and a special commissioner appointed by the Congressional Commission to investigate into the circumstances surrounding the assassination of the president.[3] A second portion of the same document gives a succession of questions put to Arnold as to his life, etc. by the notary public.

At that time the writings stopped for many years, but in the early nineties Mr. Arnold began the task of writing the entire story of his life. With painstaking efforts he placed in black and white a graphic story, dealing with the entire subject at hand, and recorded events that to the mind of the present seem too terrible to be real. The clear cut, even and legible calligraphy, together with the nature of the subject matter, with its plainly carefully weighed, yet pointed contraction, all give a key to the character of the writer.

After his release from the Dry Tortugas, Arnold seeking seclusion and retirement, dropped from the public eye and eyes in Baltimore but little was known of him in recent years. Until six years ago he resided in this city, and to those who did find him he always refused to open his lips. The knowledge that he had prepared a statement of his experiences to be given out after his death was prevalent in a narrow circle at first, and gradually, without even knowing where Arnold was to be found, it extended to other parts of the country.

Recalled by a Death.

Some weeks ago another Samuel Arnold died in Anne Arundel county, Md. and the story was erroneously published in some parts of the country that the Arnold of the Lincoln conspiracy had passed away.[4] Telegrams immediately reached *The American* from every part of the country asking that the last statement of Arnold be forwarded to various papers, and this produced inquiries which led to the establishment of the fact that Samuel Bland Arnold was still alive, living quietly on a farm in an out-of-the-way portion of Maryland.

Sam Arnold's home near Friendship, Md.

Of the eight men who, according to the story of Arnold, conspired together to abduct President Lincoln, but two now live --- Arnold and Mr. John H. Surratt, who now lives in this city.[5] Mr. Surratt is the son of Mrs. Mary E. Surratt, who was one of those hanged in the arsenal at Washington for alleged complicity in the murder of the martyred president, and who is now generally looked upon as having been innocent of the crime for which she suffered the death penalty.[6]

John Wilkes Booth, the assassin of Lincoln, was shot and killed when captured in a barn in Northern Virginia. David E. Herold, who was captured with him, and Lewis Payne[7] and George A. Atzerodt, went to their death on the scaffold with Mrs. Surratt. Samuel B. Arnold, Dr. Samuel A. Mudd, Michael O'Laughlin and Edward Spangler were tried for the murder of the president with the others, and were sentenced to life imprisonment in the Dry Tortugas. Arnold alone lives of these men, all of whom were pardoned by President Johnson in 1869.[8]

Surratt, the only other living conspirator, according to

the story of Arnold, fled the country after the assassination of President Lincoln. Surratt was in Elmira, N.Y. when the assassination took place, and he vanished from sight in spite of the utmost endeavors of government detectives to arrest him, and was not heard of again for two years. Without a cent in his pocket Surratt, with an unknown companion, reached St. Albans, Vt. and then walked to Franklin, on the other side of the line.

Surratt in Canada.

Once having found an asylum in Canada, Surratt received funds and remained in Montreal for some time. Feeling that he could not remain secreted with the American detectives swarming in Canada, Surratt took passage for England, and from there went to Rome. He enlisted in the Papal Zouaves, and was arrested while in that command. Surratt broke loose from his captors and fled, and finally reached Naples.

At Naples he succeeded in shipping aboard a fishing sloop bound for Messina, and reached Alexandria by that means. His purpose was, after reaching Cairo, to make his way to Upper Egypt, where he would be away from the touch of civilization. The American consul at Cairo, however, was on the outlook, and Surratt was again arrested soon after his arrival there. He was sent home on the United States steamer *Swatara*, returned to Washington, tried, and was not convicted. The two years which had elapsed since his flight had calmed down public indignation, and he was neither executed nor had to suffer the same punishment as those of his alleged confederates, who were sent to the Dry Tortugas.

That Arnold had no part in the actual assassination, he having left Washington some time previous, and having been employed at Old Point Comfort as a clerk, when that great crime was committed, has long since received practical acknowledgement at the hands of the public, and in his statement now given out, he tells what he says in the entire and true story of the affair as far as his knowledge extends. Knowledge of a plan to assassinate President Lincoln he confines to Booth, Payne, Atzerodt, and Herold, and holds Mrs. Surratt as entirely guiltless of the crime of which she was charged, and for which she suffered the death penalty.

"The Dry Tortugas a Hell."

Probably the most remarkable portion of the story of

Arnold, as told by himself, is the recital of cruelties practiced upon himself and other prisoners of the government, as well as to soldiers themselves at the Dry Tortugas, which he describes as a veritable hell on earth. These events, he says, he recorded from day to day in a diary, from which his manuscript in full was compiled.[9]

The story of the cruelties as set down by Arnold in his diary received the support of Dr. Samuel A. Mudd in a letter which is reproduced with this publication. Mr. Arnold wishes it distinctly understood that this relates only to those things enumerated as having taken place during the confinement of Dr. Mudd and himself in the Dry Tortugas. "Personally," said Mr.Arnold in this regard, "I never saw nor knew Mudd prior to our trial. To that period he was totally unknown to me, and therefore I would not have his name brought forward in any manner as to any connection with that portion of my statement covering the abduction plot. Honor forbids a thought that would drag innocence into my story. Of Dr. Mudd I know nothing whatever, beyond our association as fellow political prisoners. He is now dead. He bore his sufferings the same as I. Let his departed spirit rest, which I hope may be my case, after my statement has been made public to the world, the trouble never again to be resurrected."

The letter of Dr. Mudd is as follows:

Fort Jefferson, Fla.
November 25, 1865

I have read the statement in regard to the treatment of Arnold, O'Laughlin, Spangler, Colonel Grenfell and Mudd, and all representations are substantially correct.

Very respectfully, etc.
SAMUEL A. MUDD

A Fateful Letter.

Arnold's arrest was brought about by the circumstance of the finding of a letter in the trunk of John Wilkes Booth, after the assassination, of which Arnold later speaks at length in his manuscript. While at the time this letter was seized upon by the prosecution as strong evidence against Arnold, it will probably be regarded in the future as supporting Arnold's claim that his part alone was in the conspiracy to abduct Lincoln, and that he had even practically abandoned the idea of this, and that the letter was intended to dissuade Booth from that scheme.

The letter as recorded at the trial, was as follows:[10]

Hookstown, Baltimore County,
March 27, 1865

Dear John:

Was business so important that you could not remain in Baltimore till I saw you? I came in as soon as I could, but found you had gone to W---n. I called also to see Mike, but learned from his mother he had gone out with you, and had not returned. I concluded, therefore, he had gone with you. How inconsiderate you have been! When I left you, you stated we would not meet in a month or so. Therefore, I made application for employment, an answer to which I shall receive during the week. I told my parents I had ceased with you. Can I, then, under existing circumstances, come as you request? You know full that the G---t suspicions something is going on there: therefore, the undertaking is becoming more complicated. Why not, for the present, desist, for various reasons, which if you look into, you can readily see, without my making any mention thereof.

Suspicions Aroused.

You, or anyone, can censure me for my present course. You have been its cause, for how can I now come after telling them I had left you? Suspicion rests upon me now, for my whole family, and even parties in the county. I will be compelled to leave my home anyhow, and how soon, I care not. None, no not one, were more in favor of the enterprise than myself, and today would be there, had you not done as you have -- by this I mean, manner of proceeding. I am, as you will know, in need. I am, you may say, in rags, whereas, today I ought to be well clothed. I do not feel right stalking about with means, and more from appearances a beggar. I feel my dependence, but even all this would and was forgotten, for I was one with you. Time more propitious will arrive.

Do not act rashly or in haste. I would prefer your first query, go and see how it will be taken in R---d, and ere long I shall be better prepared to again be with you. I dislike writing; would sooner verbally make known my views; yet your non-writing causes me thus to proceed.

Do not in anger peruse this. Weigh all I have said, and, as a rational man and a friend, you cannot censure or upbraid my conduct. I sincerely trust this, nor aught else that shall or may occur, will ever be an obstacle to obliterate our former friendship and attachment. Write me to Baltimore, as I expect to be in about Wednesday or Thursday, or, if you can possibly come on, I will Tuesday meet you in Baltimore, at B---. Ever I subscribe myself,

Your friend,

SAM.

Approval of Sentence.

When the commission found Arnold guilty he was sentenced to imprisonment at hard labor for life, at such place as the president should direct. President Johnson approved the findings of the commission in regard to the execution of Herold, Atzerodt, Payne, and Mrs. Surratt, and of imprisonment for the others in the following words:

"The foregoing sentences in the cases of David E. Herold, G.A. Atzerodt, Lewis Payne, Michael O'Laughlin, Edward Spangler, Samuel Arnold, Mary E. Surratt and Samuel A. Mudd are hereby approved, and it is ordered that the sentences of said David E. Herold, G.A. Atzerodt, Lewis Payne, and Mary E. Surratt be carried into execution by the proper military authority, under the direction of the Secretary of War, on the 7th day of July, 1865, between the hours of 10 o'clock A.M. and 2 o'clock P.M. of that day. It is further ordered that the prisoners, Samuel Arnold, Samuel A. Mudd, Edward Spangler and Michael O'Laughlin be confined at hard labor in the penitentiary at Albany, New York, during the period designated in their respective sentences."

The above approval was made on July 5, 1865, and 10 days later President Johnson modified the order so that the prisoners be confined at the Dry Tortugas instead of at the Albany penitentiary. As will be seen by the story of Arnold, this change had a deep after significance to the life prisoners.

Chapter Two

—

ASSASSINATION OF PRESIDENT LINCOLN

—

Booth's Crime, His Escape and Death.

—

Blame Carried to High Confederate Officials.

—

*Confederacy Exonerated---Booth Found in a Barn
Rebel Officials Blamed by Johnson*

[Sunday, December 7, 1902]

President Lincoln was shot on the night of the 14th of April, 1865, while at Ford's Theatre, in Washington, to witness the production of "The American Cousin."[1] The chief executive of the nation lingered until 22 minutes past 7 o'clock on the morning of April 15, 1865, when death came.

While the second scene of the third act was being performed the audience was startled by hearing the discharge of a pistol, Booth having entered the box, and while standing between the door and the President, fired the fatal shot, with an exclamation which is said to have been "Freedom." Major Henry R. Rathbone, who was in the box, grappled with Booth, but the actor wrenched himself from his grasp and at the same time wounded that officer in the left arm with a knife.

Booth rushed to the front of the box and leaped over the railing to the stage. In jumping Booth used a flag hanging by the box to aid himself in the leap, crying at the time "Sic semper tyrannis". The assassin ran out the back door of the theater, where a horse was in waiting, and although his leg had been broken, made good his escape for the time.[2]

When those in the box had time to realize what had happened the President was found to be unconscious. The outer door of the passage way had been barred with a heavy piece of plank by Booth, and persons outside were unable to get in until this obstruction was removed by Major Rathbone. The President was carried from the theater, and Mrs. Lincoln, who was intensely excited, was assisted from the playhouse. Neither Mrs. Lincoln nor Miss Harris,[3] who was present in the box, noticed Booth until he fired the shot.

Abraham Lincoln

Confederacy Exonerated.

During his story Arnold takes upon his own shoulders, in conjunction with Booth, Atzerodt, Payne, O'Laughlin, Herold, Surratt, and Spangler, the entire responsibility of a number of plots to abduct or kidnap President Lincoln, and he exonerates from all complicity in these plots, or in the assassination, which he described as but the product of a few hours, the Confederate States government or its higher officials. During the trial the prosecution endeavored to bring out statements to that end, and the early histories of Lincoln and of his untimely end give wide credence to this theory.[4]

In that portion of "The Life of Abraham Lincoln," by Joseph H. Barrett, commissioner of pensions, published in 1865, dealing with the death of Lincoln, the trend of the opinions of that time in government circles in Washington is probably as well shown as anywhere else. A portion of this publication is as follows:[5]

"The assassination of Abraham Lincoln was the culmination of a series of fiendish schemes undertaken in the aid of an infamous rebellion. It was the deadly flower of the rank and poisonous weed of treason. The guiding and impelling spirits of secessionism nerved and aimed the blow struck by the barbarous and cowardly assassin, who stole up from behind to surprise his victim, and brutally murdered him in the privacy of his box and in the presence of his wife.

"Large rewards were speedily offered for the capture of the chief assassin and of his principal known accomplices, Atzerodt and Herold. The villain who attempted the murder of Mr. Seward was first arrested -- giving his name as Payne. Booth and his accomplice, Herold, were traced through the counties of Prince Georges, Charles and St. Mary's, Md., and finally across the Potomac, in King George and Caroline counties, in Virginia.

Found in a Barn.

"They had crossed the Rappahannock at Port Conway and had advanced some distance toward Bowling Green. By the aid of information obtained from negroes, and from a rebel paroled prisoner, they were finally found in a barn on a Mr. Garrett's place early in the morning of the 26th of April, when Herold surrendered. Booth, defiant to the last, was shot by Sergt. Boston Corbett, of the cavalry force in pursuit of the fugitives, and lived but a few hours, ending his life in miserable agony. In leaping from the box of the theater he had broken a bone of his leg, impeding his flight and producing intense suffering during the 11 days of his wanderings.

"In addition to the arrests of Payne and Herold were those of Atzerodt, O'Laughlin, Spangler, an employe at Ford's Theater; Dr. Mudd, who harbored Booth the day after the assassination, set the broken bone of his leg and helped him on his way; Arnold, whose letter to Booth, found in the latter's trunk, signed "Sam," showed his connection with the conspiracy, and Mrs. Surratt, at whose house some of the conspirators were wont to meet, and who was charged with aiding the escape of Booth.

Rebel Officials Blamed.

"But the conspiracy was clearly traceable to a higher source than Booth and these wretched accomplices. Mr. Johnson, who had been inaugurated as president on the morning of Mr. Lincoln's death, issued after the plot had become more fully unraveled, the following:

`Whereas it appears from the evidence of the Bureau of Military Justice that the atrocious murder of the late President Lincoln and the attempted assassination of the Hon. W.H. Seward, Secretary of State, were incited, concerted and procured by and between Jefferson Davis, late of Richmond, Va., and Jacob Thompson, Clement C. Clay, Beverly Tucker, George N. Sanders, W. C. Cleary and other rebels and traitors against the government of the United States, harbored in Canada; now therefore, to the end that justice may be done, I, Andrew Johnson, President of the United States, do offer and promise for the arrest of said persons, or either of them, within the limits of the United States, so that they can be brought to trial, the following rewards: One hundred thousand dollars for the arrest of Jefferson Davis, $25,000 for the arrest of Clement C. Clay, $25,000 for the arrest of Jacob Thompson, late of Mississippi, $25,000 for the arrest of George N. Sanders, $25,000 for the arrest of Beverly Tucker and $10,000 for the arrest of William C. Cleary, late clerk of Clement C. Clay.

`The Provost Marshal General of the United States is directed to cause a description of said persons, with notice of the above rewards, to be published.

`In testimony whereof I have hereunto set my hand and caused the seal of the United States to be affixed.

`Done at the city of Washington the 2d day of May, in the year of our Lord, one thousand eight hundred and sixty-five, and of the independence of the United States of America the eighty ninth.

ANDREW J0HNSON.
`By the President,
W. Hunter
acting secretary of state.'[6]

Chapter Three

—

FUTILE EFFORTS TO SAVE MRS. SURRATT

—

President Johnson's Refusal to Stay Execution Belief in Unfortunate Woman's Innocence.

—

Gen. Hartranft's Plea for Reprieve---Hopes Dashed on Bayonets---The Final Failure to Obtain Clemency---Gen. Hancock Sees A Tearstained Face---Some Political After Effects of the Execution

[Sunday, December 7, 1902]

Great interest has always centered about the case of Mrs. Mary E. Surratt, and there are many firm believers in her innocence of any criminal knowledge concerning the assassination plot. In years after the close of the war, when the bitterness of that great strife had passed away, much publicity was given her case from time to time, and many of those who were connected with the trial in official capacity were made the centers of attack.

Mr. John P. Brophy, who was at the time of the trial an instructor at Gonzaga College, in Washington, had an interesting experience in endeavoring to aid Mrs. Surratt. After her conviction for complicity in the murder, Weichman,[1] who boarded in her house and was the chief witness against her, came to him and said that in spite of all he had sworn to, he thoroughly believed Mrs. Surratt was innocent of all knowledge of the plot against the president until after its actual consummation. Mr. Brophy deemed Weichman's statement so important that he reduced it to writing and sent it to President Johnson as at least worthy of investigation.

To his communication he got no reply, but on the night before the execution he received from the War Department a permit to visit Mrs. Surratt in the arsenal where, with the three other condemned prisoners, she was confined. Mr. Brophy had not asked for any such permit, and he has always supposed that Mrs. Surratt heard of his action on her behalf and herself made the request that he be allowed to see her.

Met Mrs. Surratt.

Mr. Brophy went to the arsenal. Mrs. Surratt asked him to undertake at some future time, when the passions of the war were cooled, the task of clearing her name of the crime for which she then stood condemned and of which she earnestly protested her innocence. This Mr. Brophy promised to do. After leaving her he went to see Lewis Payne Powell, known throughout the conspiracy as Lewis Payne. Powell, who was the son of a Florida clergyman, was, after Booth, the fiercest and most bloodthirsty of all the conspirators. He retained to the last a stoical cynicism which he had shown from the first. In this mood Mr. Brophy found him a few hours before he was hanged.

To his own impending fate he told Mr. Brophy he was utterly indifferent. He had played his part in the tragedy and was ready to take the consequences of an act which he in no way regretted.

Mary E. Surratt

But when he spoke of Mrs. Surratt all trace of affectation disappeared. That woman, he protested by all that he held most sacred, was innocent of the plot against Mr. Lincoln as the child unborn. Powell's manner was so earnest and so convincing that it made a profound impression upon Mr. Brophy.

It was now about 9 o'clock in the morning. The execution was to take place between 11 A.M. and 1 P.M. Mr. Brophy from Powell's cell, hurried straight to General Hartranft, afterward governor of Pennsylvania, and then the provost marshal general having full charge of the assassins.[2] He earnestly besought General Hartranft to go to Powell and hear what he had to say. This General Hartranft did and came back impressed quite as Mr. Brophy had been:

"I will furnish you an army conveyance and swift horses," he said. "Take it and drive like mad to the White House and give the President this note. I will delay the execution until the last moment or until I hear from you definitely and positively what the President's answer is."

Plea for Reprieve.

The note was a strong plea for a reprieve for Mrs. Surratt. With it in his pocket Mr. Brophy drove on a gallop to the White House. Here, about the first person he saw was Miss Anna Surratt, daughter of the condemned woman, who for hours had been at the Executive Mansion trying to get access to the President to plead for her mother's life.

Two men barred the way to all who wished to get at President Johnson. These were Preston King and Gen. James Lane. President Johnson was suspected of having a vacillating nature, and those who believed that justice had been done in the conviction of the conspirators did not want an appeal to the weak side of the President's character to succeed.

Mr. Brophy tried to get past the guards, but tried in vain. He tried to get General Hartranft's note sent in to the President.

In that also he failed. After nearly an hour's delay he was no nearer doing his errand of life and death than when he first arrived. His own half-distracted frame of mind was intensified by the frantic entreaties of Miss Surratt, who, sobbing and choking with grief, was clinging to him and begging him to do something.

But what could he do? In every avenue that led toward the President there was a gleaming bayonet and behind the bayonet the stern bronzed face of a soldier. Mr. Brophy was at the verge of despair when suddenly a fine carriage came dashing up to the White House entrance and out of it hurried a richly dressed and strikingly handsome woman, the beautiful Mrs. Stephen A. Douglas, wife of Lincoln's old-time rival out in Illinois, the Little Giant.

Dashed on Bayonets.

Mrs. Douglas, too, had come to plead Mrs. Surratt's case.

Mr. Brophy was by her side in an instant telling her his errand and entreating her to get him access to the President. Mrs. Douglas was a woman of resolution and furthermore a dazzlingly beautiful woman. She dashed straight at the bayonets and they lowered almost in homage before her.

The civilian guards beyond the bayonets tried to stop her, but she swept them scornfully aside with an imperious gesture. What no one else in all that crucial forenoon could do was precisely the thing which Mrs. Douglas did. She got to the President.

But there her triumph ceased. She entered the room with her face flushed with energy and hope. She came out of it with bitter, hopeless disappointment in her every feature and every movement. She looked at the convulsed, tear-stained face of the young girl whose mother's life was trembling in the balance and could only shake her head.

"Oh, don't give up so!" sobbed Miss Surratt. "Don't! Don't! Oh, do go to him again. He won't refuse you. He can't. Do go to him again!"

"Show him General Hartranft's note again," cried Mr. Brophy. "Ask him if he got the statement I sent him of Weichmann's confession to me. Make another appeal to him, Mrs. Douglas."

"I will," said the spirited woman. "I will. It is of little use, though. I feel that it is of little use."

The Final Failure.

Past the bayonets, past the guards, she once more forced her way to the President's presence. But she had predicted truly when she said that it was of little use. There was no vacillation in Johnson now. He firmly and positively refused to intervene. The statement of Weichmann, he said, had come to him. It was wholly without weight. With this reply, Mrs. Douglas came back.

"We have done what we could, Miss Surratt," said Mr. Brophy to the half-dazed girl. "Come with me if you would see your mother again while she lives."

So into the army carriage waiting at the door Miss Surratt and Mr. Brophy got and again there was a mad gallop through the Washington streets. They were all but deserted. For all of Washington at that hour there was just one magnet -- the arsenal, where Lincoln's murder was to be avenged.[5]

The crowd that surged around the building reached blocks away and was impenetrable. Mr. Brophy's carriage was brought up sharply at its outer borders. It was a complete blockade. There was no budging an inch.

Meantime, the minutes were flying. The time which would mark the limit when mother and daughter never would meet again this side of the grave was close at hand. For Miss Surratt and her companion it was a moment of agony as trying as the long wait at the President's door. Once more it seemed a case for sheer despair and once more a carriage came dashing up to the rescue.

A Tearstained Face.

There was a clattering of horses' hoofs, and when Mr. Brophy turned in the direction from which it came he saw a guard of cavalry galloping on each side of a swiftly moving carriage, in which appeared the handsome, soldierly face of General Hancock, then the general in command at Washington.[4] The General saw the confusion about Brophy's carriage, recognized the army vehicle and saw the tear-stained, distracted face of a woman.

He brought his cavalcade to an instant halt. Then he left his own carriage, walked to that of Miss Surratt, and hat in hand and with the chivalrous dignity which sat so well upon him, asked what the trouble was and what he could do. Mr. Brophy briefly explained that it was Miss Surratt trying to speak to her mother once more on earth. The soldier's face flushed and Mr. Brophy is sure there was something very like tears in his eyes as he grasped the pathetic situation.

"Poor child!" he said gently, and then beckoned an officer to him and gave to him an order. Then he returned to his own carriage and the squadron of cavalry formed about both carriages. A lane through the crowd was quickly cut and Miss Surratt reached the arsenal and her mother's side in time to bid her a last good-by.

After the execution Miss Surratt went to live with Mr. and Mrs. Brophy, and was married from their house some years afterward.[5]

Some After Effects.

When General Hancock was a candidate for the Democratic nomination for the presidency many Southern delegates opposed him, believing that he had been harsh in his measures in reference to Mrs. Surratt. Mr. Brophy went to General Hancock's friends and volunteered to make a statement of the general's action above related as well as of the fact that on the morning of the execution the General had posted a mounted cavalryman on every block between the arsenal and the White House, with orders to bear a reprieve, in case one came for Mrs. Surratt, in relays and at top speed to General Hartranft. With the publication of this statement Southern opposition to General Hancock ceased.[6]

Mrs. Surratt was a Catholic, and when General Hartranft ran for governor of Pennsylvania, the fact that he was the provost marshal general in Washington at the time of the execution was used in an effort to unite Catholic opposition to him. Mr. Brophy was on a lecturing tour in Pennsylvania at the time and his narration of the incident of the note to President Johnson and the delayed execution did much to break down this particular scheme on the part of the General's opponents.

A curious climax to the story of that tragic morning in Washington is the fact that Preston King, one of the men who headed off those who would have pleaded with the president for Mrs. Surratt, committed suicide by filling his pockets full of shot and jumping off a North River ferryboat in New York, while the other, General Lane, committed suicide by blowing out his brains somewhere in a Western state.[7]

Chapter Four

—

ARNOLD'S NARRATIVE TO BEGIN TOMORROW.

—

Serial Publication Will Run Daily and Sunday Until Concluded -- Comprises 30,000 Words

—

Arnold's Story Begins---Booth Had Large Income---Early Preparations---
A Mother's Dreams---The Parts Alotted---Another Plan Hatched---Conspiracy
Abandoned---Surratt in Richmond---Arnold Placed Under Arrest.

[Monday, December 8, 1902]

The statement of Arnold consists of about 30,000 words, or about 25 columns of matter. This has been divided into 13 chapters, which The *American* will publish in serial form, beginning tomorrow. These publications will continue daily and Sunday until the series is completed.

The publication will bear the caption: "Lincoln Conspiracy and the Conspirators."

The narrative as set forth by Mr. Arnold contains some startling revelations. Arnold is their author, and they will be furnished exclusively to the readers of The *American* for what they are worth.

Arnold's Story Begins.

Samuel Bland Arnold begins his life story by telling of his meeting with Booth in September, 1864, and thus leading on up to the plots to kidnap President Lincoln, detailing all of the attendant circumstances. The statement was sworn to before a notary public at Dry Tortugas, Fla., on December 3, 1867, and the conditions under which it was drawn up, with its significance are dealt with by Mr. Arnold in his general statement to follow.

The following is a full text of the document:[1]

It was in the latter part of August, or about the first part of September, A.D. 1864, that J. Wilkes Booth, hearing I was in town, sent word to me that he would like to see me at Barnum's Hotel in the City of Baltimore, at which place he was then stopping. I had not seen Booth since the year 1852, at which time we were fellow students at St. Timothy's Hall, Catonsville, Md., the Revd. L. Van Bokkelen being then President of said Institute. I called upon him and was kindly received as an old schoolmate and invited to his room. We conversed together, seated by a table smoking a cigar, of past hours of youth, and the present war, said he had heard I had been south, &c, when a tap at the door was given and O'Laughlin was ushered into the room. O'Laughlin was a former acquaintance of Booths from boyhood up, so he informed me. I was introduced to him and this was my first acquaintance with O'Laughlin.

Samuel B. Arnold, 1865

In a short time wine was called for by Booth and we drank and freely conversed together about the war, the present condition of the South and in regard to the non-exchange of prisoners. Booth then spoke of the abduction or kidnapping of the President, saying if such could be accomplished and the President taken to Richmond and held as a hostage, he thought it would bring about an exchange of prisoners. He said the President frequently went to the Soldiers Home alone and unguarded, that he could be easily captured on one of these visits, and carried to the Potomac, boated across the river and conveyed to Richmond.

These were the ideas advanced by Booth and he alone was the moving spirit. After a debate of some time and his pointing out its feasibility and being under the effects of some little of wine, we consented to join him in the enterprise. We alone comprised the entire party to this scheme at that time as far as my knowledge extends. We separated that afternoon and I returned to my brother's near Hookstown, Baltimore County, Md. Booth stating he would leave for New York the next day to wind up his affairs and make over his property to different members of his family, reserving enough to carry out his projected scheme and would soon return.

Had Large Income.

Booth said he would furnish all the necessary materials to carry out the project. He showed me the different entries in his diary of what his engagements paid him in his profession and I judged from what I have heard his income therefrom to be from $25,000.00 to $30,000.00. He also informed me he owned property in the oil regions of Pennsylvania and Boston. He was taken sick while at home and upon his secrecy he arranged his business and went to the oil regions from which place he wrote me enclosing twenty dollars for expenses, requesting me to look around and pick out a horse for him.[2]

This is all the money I ever received from Booth or any other person in connection with this undertaking. He went from the oil regions to Canada and shipped his wardrobe to Nassau as he afterwards informed me. Booth returned to Baltimore some time in November or December 1864. He had purchased whilst North some arms to defend himself in case of pursuit, viz: 2 carbines, 3 Pairs Revolvers, 3 Knives and two pairs of Hand cuffs. Fearful that the weight of his trunk might attract attention, he asked me to take part of them, which I did and sent them to him by express to Washington.

A short time after his return from Canada to Baltimore he went to the lower counties of Maryland bordering on the Potomac as he said for the purpose of purchasing horses and boats.[3] I met him in Baltimore in January, I think at which time he purchased a buggy and harness and now said that all was completed and ready to go to work. I informed my parents I was in the oil business with Booth to prevent them from knowing the true cause of my association with Booth. O'Laughlin and myself drove the buggy to Washington; this was some time in the latter part of December 1864 or early part of January 1865.

Early Preparations.

We left the horse at Nailor's Livery Stable on the Avenue near 13th Street, and we went to Rullman's Hotel[4] (kept by Lichau) on Pennsylvania Avenue. We remained there a few days and then went to Mitchell's Hotel near Grover's Theatre and remained a few days. We went from there and rented a room from Mrs. Van Tyne, No. 420 D Street and obtained our meals at Franklin Hotel at the corner of D & 8th Streets, and there remained off and on until the 20th of March 1865, during which time I frequently went to Baltimore (nearly every Saturday). O'Laughlin as a general thing always went and returned with me on these visits.

When in Baltimore I remained at my father's. When in Washington I spent most of my time at Rullman's Hotel (kept by Lichau) on Pennsylvania Avenue at which place O'Laughlin and myself had acquaintances.

The President having ceased visiting the Soldiers Home, Booth proposed a plan to abduct him from the theatre, by carrying him back off the stage by the back entrance, place him in a buggy which he was to have in attendance and during the confusion which would be produced by turning off the gas, make good our escape. I objected to any such arrangement and plainly pointed out its utter impracticability and told Booth it could not be accomplished. He would listen to no argument I could bring forth and seemed resolved in carrying out this mad scheme. He endeavored to obtain a man from New York to turn off the gas, in this he failed, so he informed me.[5]

This was in the latter part of January, 1865 or early part of February, 1865. Booth at this time was stopping at the National Hotel. About this time I called at his room, accompanied by O'Laughlin and upon entering was introduced to Surratt under the name I think of Cole. This was about 10 or 11 o'clock A.M. and Booth was still in bed. This was the first time I ever met Surratt. Surratt left a few moments after we came in, and Booth informed us he was one of the parties engaged in the abduction and his name was Surratt.

A Mother's Dreams.

About this time Booth told me he had received a letter from his mother in which she stated she had fearful dreams about him. She sent his brother Junius Brutus to Washington to persuade him to come home, so Booth told me. Booth told me he did not wish his brother to know how many horses he had as he knew his brother would ask an explanation why he kept so many. He asked me then to go down to Cleaver's Stable and I did so. He told Mr. Cleaver I had purchased the horse and he was turned over to me.[6]

John Wilkes Booth

About a week afterwards I went to the stable, paid the livery on the horse and rode him up to the corner of D and 8th Streets and turned him over either to O'Laughlin or Booth and I never saw the horse afterwards. Booth afterwards repaid me for the board of the horse.

Booth was absent from the city of Washington the best part of the month of February. On his return he stated he had been to New York. On the night of the 15th of March, 1865 about 12 or 12.30 at night as O'Laughlin and myself were about leaving Rullman's Hotel, Penna. Avenue (kept by Lichau) on our way to our room Booth sent a messenger (Herold) who at that time was unknown to me requesting us to accompany Herold to Gotier's Eating Saloon.[7] Herold I learned from O'Laughlin had been introduced to him that day by Booth during their buggy ride.

We accordingly went up and were ushered into the room where seated around a table were Booth, Surratt, Atzerodt alias Port Tobacco, and Payne alias Mosby, all of whom with the exception of Booth and Surratt I had never seen or heard of before. We were then formally introduced. Oysters, liquors and cigars were obtained. Booth then remarked these were the parties engaged to assist in the abduction of the President.

Whereupon the plan of abducting him from the theatre was introduced and discoursed upon, Booth saying if it could not be done from the lower box, it could from the upper one.

The Parts Allotted.

He set forth the part he wished each one to perform. He and Payne alias Mosby were to seize him in the box. O'Laughlin and Herold to put out the gas. I was to jump upon the stage and assist them as he was lowered down from the box. Surratt and Atzerodt alias Port Tobacco were to be on the other side of the Eastern Branch Bridge to act as pilots and to assist in conveying him to the boats which had been purchased by Booth. Booth said everything was in readiness.

The gist of the conversation during the meeting was whether it could or could not be accomplished in the manner as proposed. After listening to Booth and the others' comments I firmly protested and objected to the whole scheme, and told them of its utter impracticability. I stated that prisoners were now being exchanged and the object to be obtained by the abduction had been accomplished, that patriotism was the motive that prompted me in joining in the scheme, not ambition. That I wanted a shadow of a chance for my life and I intended having it.

Then an angry discussion arose between Booth and myself in which he threatened to shoot me. I told him two could play at that game and before them all expressed my firm determination to have nothing more to do with it after that week. About 5 o'clock in the morning the meeting broke up and O'Laughlin and myself went to our room at Mrs. Van Tyne's.

The next day as I was standing in front of Rullman's Hotel, Penna Avenue (kept by Lichau) in company with O'Laughlin, Booth riding by on horseback stopped and called O'Laughlin. He conversed with him a short time and returned saying Booth wanted to see me. I went to the curb and met him. Booth apologized to me for the words he had used at the meeting, remarking he thought I must have been drunk in making the objections I did at the meeting in reference to his proposed plan of carrying out the abduction. I told him no! drunkenness was on his and his party's part, that I was never more sober in my life and what I said last night I meant and that this week should end my connection in the affair.

Another Plan Hatched.

On the 17th day of March, 1865 about 2 o'clock Booth

and Herold met O'Laughlin and myself. Booth stated he was told the President was going to attend a theatrical performance out on 7th Street at a soldiers encampment or hospital at the outer edge of the city.[8] Booth had previously sent a small black box (containing 2 carbines, a monkey wrench, ammunition & a piece of rope, by the porter of the National Hotel to our room at Mrs. Van Tyne's. Not wishing it to remain in our room O'Laughlin sent the box to an acquaintance of his in Washington. This box was sent to our room in the early part of March, I think, and was removed in about a week or ten days.

After Booth and Herold met O'Laughlin and myself and made arrangements to go out to the performance on 7th Street, Booth, Herold, and O'Laughlin went for the box containing the 2 carbines &c. The understanding was that Herold was to take the box with Booth's horse and buggy to either Surrattsville or T.B. and there meet us in case the abduction was successful. This was the last time I saw Herold until our trial.

O'Laughlin returned and we took our dinner at the Franklin Hotel as usual. After dinner we met Booth and accompanied him to a livery stable near the Patent Office at which place Booth obtained horses for us. O'Laughlin and myself rode to our room on D Street and made all our necessary arrangements each arming himself. O'Laughlin and myself rode out to where the performance was to take place.

We stopped at a restaurant at the foot of the hill to await the arrival of the other parties. They not arriving as soon as we expected, we remounted our horses and rode out the road about a mile. We there returned and stopped at the same restaurant. Whilst in there Atzerodt came in who had just arrived with Payne. A short time after Booth and Surratt came in and we drank together. Booth made enquiries at the encampment at which place the performance was to be held and learned he, the President, was not there. After telling us this we separated, O'Laughlin, Payne, and myself riding back to the city together. Surratt and Booth rode out the road towards the country. O'Laughlin and myself left our horses back of the National Hotel at a livery stable.[9]

Conspiracy Abandoned.

About 8 o'clock, I met Booth and Surratt near the stable. This was the last time I ever saw Surratt and I never saw Payne after we parted in our ride to the city until the day of our trial. O'Laughlin and myself left Washington on the 20th of March and went to Baltimore. Booth went to New York and thus I thought the whole affair abandoned. I then told my family I had ceased business in Washington and severed my connections with Booth.

Father told me if I would apply to J.W. Wharton for employment I might obtain it as Wharton was looking for a clerk the last time he came up from Old Point Comfort, Va. to Baltimore. I went out to my brother's at Hookstown, Baltimore County and I returned March the 25th to Baltimore. I was informed at my father's that Booth had called to see me and left a card requesting me to call upon him at Barnum's Hotel. I found a letter there also from him for me, in which he stated he desired to give it another trial the week following and if unsuccessful to abandon it forever. The letter found in Booth's trunk was in answer to the letter which I innocently wrote to prevent his undertaking it.

George and Mary Jane Arnold, Sam's parents

On the same day, March 27, 1865 I applied to J.W. Wharton at Old Point Comfort for employment and received a favorable answer to my application on the 31st March 1865. O'Laughlin came to my father's to which place I had returned from my brothers and requested me to accompany him to Washington to see Booth for the purpose of obtaining $500.00 which Booth had borrowed of him. I went with him that morning and returned with him in the early afternoon train of the same day. At the depot at Washington we accidentally met Atzerodt. We drank and parted with him. I never saw him from the 17th March until then and never afterwards until our trial.

Surratt in Richmond.

We saw Booth. During our conversation he told us the President was not in Washington, he also said that Surratt had gone to Richmond, as he had understood through Weichman that a Mrs. Slater had arrived from Canada with despatches and that the party who had been in the habit of ferrying persons across the river had been arrested by the Government, in consequence of which Surratt offered his services to accompany her to Richmond.[10] I asked him if he had received my letter of the 27th, he replied he had not. I asked him when the letter was received to destroy it. He told me he would.

This interview on the 31st March took place in his room at the National Hotel. (O'Laughlin, Booth and myself). He in the conversation stated that the enterprise was abandoned. He also stated he intended to return to his profession. It was at this interview and time I asked Booth what I should do with the arms I had, he told me to keep them, to sell them or do anything I chose with them. We left him at his room in the hotel about 2 o'clock P.M. and after that time I never received either a letter from him or any other communication, nor he from he, neither have I seen him since.

We returned to Baltimore in the early afternoon train. I parted with O'Laughlin and went to my father's. I there found a letter from Wharton in which he gave me employment. This was in reply to my letter to him dated 27th March 1865 applying for a situation. The next morning I went to my brother's at Hookstown, packed up my valise, preparatory to go to Wharton's. I then gave my brother a revolver and the knife. One revolver I carried with me.

My brother drove me to the city and I took the boat that evening for Old Point and commenced clerking for Mr. Wharton on my arrival there which was April 2d, 1865. This ended my connection with the conspiracy, and I heard nothing further from it not from any of the parties connected therewith. I knew nothing about the assassination until the news reached Fort Monroe, Va. by telegraph, about 12 o'clock on the morning of the 15th of April, 1865.

Placed Under Arrest.

I was arrested at Mr. Wharton's store, Old Point Comfort, Va., on the morning of April 17, 1865. The assassination of President Lincoln was never mentioned or even hinted at in my presence by Booth or any other person.

SAMUEL ARNOLD

In the presence of
    GEORGE R. ANDREWS,
    Major, Fifth United States Artillery.
    H.F. BENNERS.

I, Samuel Arnold, do solemnly swear in the presence of Almighty God that the foregoing statement, to which I have attached my name, is true in every particular and is a full and complete history of my connection with the conspiracy to abduct or kidnap President Lincoln and a history of the several parts each was assigned to perform, and that it is a true statement, as far as my knowledge extends of all facts and persons connected with the conspiracy to abduct or kidnap; that I have not attempted to conceal any of the facts relating thereto or to screen myself or any persons connected therewith, and that I had no knowledge whatever that any attempt was to be made to assassinate President Lincoln, and furthermore I will true answer make to any and all questions which may be propounded to me in relation to myself or any other person or persons which were connected or supposed to be connected either with the abduction or assassination of President Lincoln.

SAMUEL ARNOLD
Subscribed and sworn to before me this 3d day of December, 1867.
W.H. GLEASON
Notary Public.

Chapter Five

—

ARNOLD'S SWORN STATEMENT OF 1867

—

Arnold's Life---Before Meeting Booth---Dr. Mudd's Connection---No Reward for Deed---How the South Felt---Arnold Not a Knight of the Golden Circle

[Tuesday, December 9, 1902]

After making the signed and sworn statement of the last publication, Samuel B. Arnold was closely questioned by W.H. Gleason, notary public, and commissioner appointed by the Congressional Committee to investigate into the particulars concerning the assassination of President Lincoln. While, to the general reader, probably the most uninteresting portion of the entire manuscript telling the life story of Arnold, it is published in its entirety by reason of its important bearing upon subsequent portions of the writings.

The questions and answers were written on December 3, 1867, while Arnold was a state prisoner at the Dry Tortugas, Florida, and have a great interest, both through the light therein thrown on the life of Arnold and through the circumstances under which they were recorded, as told hereinafter by Arnold in a vivid description of his treatment as a prisoner and the circumstances under which the statement was made. The questioning also brought forth some of the minor details of the kidnapping plot as arranged by the conspirators, which were not adduced in the main deposition.[1]

Q: Where were you born and what is your age?
A: I was born in the District of Columbia, September 6, 1834, and I am 33 years of age.

Q: Did you ever serve in the Rebel Army?
A: Yes. I served about four months in the First Maryland Regiment, in Capt. Ned Dorsey's Company.[2] I was discharged in consequence of ill-health and returned to Maryland about September or October, 1861, and again returned after my recovery from my sickness, when the Rebel Army entered

Frederick City, Md. I followed the army back to Virginia, but did not again enlist or enter the ranks. When the army fell back toward Winchester I left and went to Richmond and immediately went from there to Augusta, Ga., at which place I had a brother stationed.[3] I went to Tullahoma, Tenn., after the battle of Murfeesboro and obtained employment as clerk with Paymaster Captain James Maurice. I stayed there until an order was issued discontinuing the employment of civilians. I then obtained employment with Captain Gibbett, Nitre and Mining Bureau, near Charleston, East Tennessee. In the month of September, 1863, I left him and returned to Augusta, Ga., and a short time afterward obtained employment with Major Bridewell, A.Q.M., in Augusta, Ga. In January, 1864, learning through a letter from home of the serious illness of my mother, I resigned my position, and, in company with a younger brother, who was employed in the office of the Nitre and Mining Bureau at Augusta, Ga., started for home.[4] I took the regular railroad route to Richmond, tried to procure a pass at General Winder's office through to the States, but could not, he stating there were no passes granted to the States. I then got a pass from the Provost Marshal for Staunton, but only went to Charlottesville. I then went through Symond's Gap into the valley. I went through Luray into Loudoun County and crossed the Potomac on the ice just above Whites Ford and then went in the City of Baltimore, where I arrived, I think, in the latter part of February, 1864. It was my intention when I left Augusta to return there again, but on my arrival I found that my mother's health was in such a critical state that to leave her again would have endangered her life.[5]

Before Meeting Booth.

Q: Where were you and what did you do after your arrival home until you met Booth?

A: I stayed at my father's in Baltimore, and my brother's, in Hookstown, off and on, until the month of June. Whilst at my brother's I assisted him on the farm.[6] About this time I learned through Dr. Morton that an expedition under Captain Fisk, of the United States Army, was fitting out for a dash and I engaged with Lieutenant Robinson to join it, and to meet him at St. Paul, Minn. I left Baltimore, I think, about the 10th of June and went direct to St. Paul. The expedition did not arrive there at the expected time, and tired of waiting and finding that my means were drawing short, I determined upon returning to Baltimore. After purchasing my ticket I saw Lieutenant Robinson and told him that I had not sufficient means to purchase my outfit. He advised me under the circumstances to return, which I did. I reached Baltimore some time in July, and from that time until I met Booth I was off and on at my father's and brother's.

Q: Did Booth make mention to you of any person or persons that he saw in Canada, or of plans or schemes which were on foot there intended to aid the South?
A: He never did.

Q: Did Booth ever inform you of his being in the South during the war?
A: He told me that he went South and showed me his pass, which I think was obtained at Vicksburg. I think it was signed by General Grant, adjutant general. He showed me the pass some time during February or March, 1865. It came out during our conversation that his object in visiting the South was a professional one and that he was to act at New Orleans.[7]

Q: Did Booth tell you that he had purchased any boats when you saw him in January?
A: I do not remember, but I know that he said everything was ready. I think he said boats were purchased.[8]

Q: Did he say he had engaged parties in lower Maryland to help him?
A: I think he told me that he had a man in charge of a boat, but did not mention his name. In conversation with Atzerodt afterward I gathered that he was the man alluded to. He mentioned no other.

Dr. Mudd's Connection.

Q: Did you ever hear Booth allude to Dr. Samuel Mudd?
A: He told me he had a letter of introduction either to Dr. Queen or Dr. Mudd, I am not sure which. He said he had been down in their neighborhood to purchase horses and had a nice

time there. That was the only time that I ever heard Booth
mention Dr. Mudd's name. That was some time in January.

Q: How did Booth propose to abduct the president from the
Soldiers' Home?
A: He intended to seize him while in his carriage and drive him
down to the Potomac, crossing the Eastern Branch bridge. I do
not know at what particular point he intended crossing the
river.

Q: With whom did you become acquainted at Rullman's Hotel,
kept by Lichau?
A: A man of the name of Purdy, Gillet, Giles, the bartender, and
some others, whose names I cannot recollect, none of whom had
any knowledge of our plans.[9]

Q: Did Booth ever say anything about his being able to procure
the assistance of anyone connected with the theater?
A: No. He said he had tried to procure a man in New York to
turn off the gas.

Q: Did Booth inform you that Surratt was in the service of the
Confederate government or was in the secrets of the persons
going to or coming from Richmond?
A: He never did.

Q: Did you know how many horses Booth had at the time he
said his brother came to see him?
A: He had three. I never saw his brother.

Q: Did Booth suggest any method by which the president could
be decoyed into an upper box?
A: He never did.

No Reward for Deed.

Q: Did you hear any of the conspirators, or any other person or
persons, speak of a reward having been offered for the assassination of President Lincoln, or that a reward would be given in
case he was killed or abducted?
A: Never did. And never read that any reward was offered for

his assassination.

Q: How was it proposed to capture the President upon the 17th of March?
A: To seize him and his carriage was the intention and to drive him round by way of Bladensburg to Surrattsville or T.B., there to meet Herold and convey him to the Potomac. It had been decided for the first attempt that ropes were to be stretched across the road for the purpose of tripping up the horses in case of pursuit. This was only in my first conversation with Booth at Barnum's Hotel.

Q: Did you ride to Mrs. Surratt's house on March 17?
A: I did not. I did not know where her house was, or that she lived in Washington. I never saw or heard of her until the day of our trial.

Q: Were there any other persons at the theatre grounds (hospital or encampment) on the 17th of March that were expecting to assist in kidnapping the President other than those mentioned in your statement?
A: There were none to my knowledge. I am positive there were no others.

Q: Do you know with whom O'Laughlin deposited the box containing the carbines?
A: I do not. I could not recall the name even if I should hear it.

Q: Did you ever hear Booth say anything about Louis F. [*sic*] Weichmann?
A: He said he had learned through Weichmann the number of prisoners that there were on both sides. I think he said those held by the United States amounted to 25,000 or 30,000.[10]

Q: On March 31, when O'Laughlin called on you and requested you to go to Washington with him, did he inform you that Booth wished to see you?
A: He did not.

How the South Felt.

Q: When you saw Booth on March 31, did he give you to understand that Surratt would consult with the authorities at Richmond and ascertain how they felt toward the abduction scheme?
A: He said nothing in regard to it, but said the whole scheme was abandoned.

Q: What did Atzerodt say about the abduction when you met him at the depot on March 31?
A: I saw Atzerodt but a few moments. He said that Booth had procured a box at the theater and that the abduction would come off that night. That is all that passed between us.

Q: Did Booth ever say to you whether any other parties in Washington or elsewhere knew of the abduction plot?
A: He never mentioned to me that any person or persons knew of it or were connected with it other than the parties we met at Gautier's upon the evening of March 15, 1865.

Q: Did you ever hear Booth say anything against Andrew Johnson?
A: Never did.

Q: Was it ever contemplated by the conspirators to abduct any member of the cabinet or any government official other than the president?
A: It never was.

Q: Did Booth ever mention anything to you about the St. Alban's Raid?
A: He said that he was either going to or coming from Canada at the time it occurred. This he told me on his arrival in Baltimore. He did not intimate that he was connected with it.

Q: Were you ever in the secret service of the Confederate government?
A: I never was.

Not Golden Circle Knight.

Q: Did you ever belong to the Order of the Knights of the

Golden Circle, or any secret society of any kind?
A: I never belonged to the Knights of the Golden Circle or any secret society of any kind.

Q: Did Booth administer any oath of secrecy to you at any time in relation to the contemplated abduction?
A: He did.

Q: Do you know of any other parties being sworn to secrecy?
A: I do not.

Q: What did O'Laughlin inform you about Booth having a commission in the Confederate service?
A: O'Laughlin told me that Booth said he had told his brother he held a commission in the Confederate Army; that his object in telling this was to prevent his brother from insisting upon going home. The brother that he referred to I supposed to be Junius Brutus.

I wish to add that I am not certain whether the letter I received from Booth containing the $20 was dated from the oil regions or from New York.

I, W.H. Gleason, do hereby certify that the foregoing is a true and correct copy of a statement, affidavit, questions and answers thereto, made by Samuel Arnold in his testimony taken before me this 3d day of December, 1867.

W.H. GLEASON

Notary public and commissioner appointed by the Congressional Committee to investigate into the particulars concerning the assassination of President Lincoln.

Chapter Six

—

IN HIS OWN WORDS

—

The Narrative Begins

—

Arnold's Background---War Changed Friendship---Left Baltimore But to Return---A Fateful Journey to the City---First Meeting With Booth---The Conspiracy Plans Outlined--No Mercenary Incentive---Booth's Canadian Visit---Booth Was a Monomaniac---Opportunities to Capture Lincoln Wasted---"Gas" Man Refused to Participate

[Wednesday, December 10, 1902]

The life story of Samuel B. Arnold remained unrecorded for many years after his pardon by President Johnson, save for that portion set down in his statement immediately after arrest in the office of Marshal McPhail, in Baltimore, and that made before W.H. Gleason, notary public, at Dry Tortugas, in 1867, and in writings compiled from testimony adduced at his trial. In the early nineties Mr. Arnold began what he avers is the true story of his entire connection with the Lincoln conspiracy and its subsequent events.

With some very slight and minor changes, the manuscript is as follows:

Twenty-five years[1] have rolled around since my return to my native state --- a free man. During that period I have silently borne both my sorrows and the many wrongs thrust upon me by overzealous writers. I declined to be interviewed by correspondents of the press, abiding my own time to give to the public any and all facts which I possessed, knowing that when I did so it would come under my own hand and everything would be truthfully transcribed. I feel it my duty not only to myself but to my country at large, to come before the public and to give as far as my knowledge extends, an authentic account of every part taken and every part known, during my connection with John Wilkes Booth.

The standard from which the history of the country is at present made up is compiled from that military inquisition,

termed a military commission, held at Washington, D.C. in the
year 1865, of which I will deal as I pursue my subject.[2]

I was born in the District of Columbia of respectable
parentage. At birth there were four traits of character which
grew stronger as age progressed. They were honor, honesty,
truthfulness and will power. It required neither law nor tutelage
to engraft them in my nature, as they were part and parcel of
my being at birth. Through life, even to my old age, they have
been just as strong and firm as in my youth. I yield to no one in
this vast country pre-eminence in these qualifications. My
parents were Christians who impressed these virtues on my
mind; beside my preceptors were men of high standing within
my native state, who both looked after my spiritual welfare and
to the observance and obedience to the governing laws of the
country.

As a youth I was wild only to enjoy the pleasures of life,
which I must say were bountiful from youth to middle age. No
wish of the heart but was gratified and life during that period
was one vast sea of pleasure. There was nothing vicious in my
nature, but I was firm and decided in all the walks of life, never
allowing anyone to impose upon me. From my birth, which
occurred in 1834,[3] I had never violated a law of the land, nor
had I violated any when arrested in 1865, although it is so
recorded that I did. Let the public disprove my assertion.

War Changed Friendship.

Fate accompanied me in all my wanderings. Through ill
health and a broken-down constitution I returned from the
South in the early part of 1864. I came ostensibly to see my
mother who was very ill. To restore her to health I promised to
remain, and I found that she gradually began to improve. My
sojourn at home was not a bed of roses. It was beyond my
mind's conception to believe, much less to feel, that the nature
of man or the feelings of the human heart could undergo so
varied a change, through civil war, as I became the witness of,
until brought into direct contact with the wide estrangement it
was productive of among those with whom from earliest years
the firmest friendship and association had existed, unmoved,
unchanged and unbroken.

It was a sorrowing sight to behold the hand so frequently
pressed in friendship's warm grasp, hang cold and listless by the
side of those whom the heart had ever cherished as one's
warmest friends. Where in former years all had been friendliness, behold, changed to hatred and bitter animosity, ready and
willing to act in concert with those whose inward dispositions

delighted in reviling and persecuting their fellow-man. That all these marked and woeful changes have been seen and bitterly and sadly felt, my marred life and racked frame bear witness of, superinduced, and, in its greatest measure, brought to its present stage through acts of basest means to my fellow-man.

Unable to cope against the swelling tide of persecution that set in upon me from every side, possessing a spirit that could nor would not brook taunting, insult, nor tamely submit to every indignity the passion of the hour felt disposed to impose and to exact, I determined to sever myself from those in whose midst I could not dwell in peace and happiness owing to the difference of political sentiments and views, and endeavor, if possible, to find in a land among strangers that just inheritance, denied me in my own native state.

Left But to Return.

Every gift of nature at my command was brought into requisition to stay and soften the evil passions engendered by the war. Fruitless and unavailing were all my efforts, and the only course left me to adopt and pursue was to seek a more congenial clime. This resolve was carried into execution during the summer of 1864, under the most trying circumstances, but was shortlived, necessity of a private nature very much against my inclination, compelling me through force of surroundings, to return to my home again in the month of July.

Thus destiny over which I had no controlling agency, nor the power to avert, forced misfortune and suffering upon me. After my return I was very guarded in both actions and speech, studiously avoiding entering into political discussions, although at periods they were forced upon me. I left the city, going to my father's country home in Baltimore county, near Hookstown, and there remained in retirement and happy contentment. Imagination could conjure up no sweeter life than this quiet country solitude, and for over a month I was truly happy.

The pleasures of the past resumed their former status in my nature; I lived over again the halcyon days passed there, when peace reigned throughout the land, e'er the rude tocsin of war marshalled foes to deluge this fair land in blood and ruin, and I was allured under the false hope into the belief that was happiness. But soon I found it was not so. The heart's yearnings could not be stifled; again restlessness took possession of my being, and the heart bounded to life again in the element of excitement, in which for three long years it had run riot.

A Fateful Journey.

The Arnold House at Hookstown

It was during my sojourn there, upon a bright and beautiful morning, during either the month of August or September, 1864, the monotony of a country life becoming very tedious and insipid, that I concluded that a short visit to the City of Baltimore would be beneficial in its effects, which thought was forthwith acceded to and carried immediately into execution, there being no plans or any object governing my actions other than to relieve the dull monotony naturally investing a country life.[4]

The morning of my arrival in the city was principally occupied in the pursuit of pleasure, accompanied by a few selected acquaintances and friends. Toward noon I returned to the residence of my father, who was residing at that period in the city, when from a younger brother, who had also been a schoolmate of John W. Booth,[5] I learned that Booth desired me to call upon him at the Barnum Hotel, at which place he was stopping.

At this period I knew nothing of John Wilkes Booth's political sentiments, nor had I the remotest idea of the result which would follow the visit. I merely called upon him as a companion and friend of my boyhood, which was most natural. I had not seen Booth since 1851, when we parted with one another at school. Separated from one another, our vocations called us to different pursuits, and he, as an individual, like the many that clustered around schoolboy days, vanished from the everyday scenes of my life. As he became eminent in his profession memory brought him back, but we never met from

1851 until that latter part of 1864.

Meeting With Booth.

The visit was made according to his request and for the first time in 13 years we looked upon each other. Fatal that meeting [was] to me, for through it the iron was entered deep into my soul and caused me to lose confidence in the human race. I found Booth possessed of wonderful power in conversation and became perfectly infatuated with his social manners and bearing. Instead of gazing upon the countenance of the mild and timid schoolmate of former years, I beheld a deep thinking man of the world before me, with highly distinguishing marks of beauty, intelligence and gentlemanly refinement, different from the common order of man, and one possessing an uninterrupted flow of conversational power, in which all the characteristics of different natures were combined.

Booth invited me to his room, where the current items of the times were freely talked over, intermingled with escapades of schoolboy days. It was not until Michael O'Laughlin, one of his earliest friends and associates in youth, had arrived and was introduced that the subject, which no doubt was uppermost in his coursing thoughts, was disclosed, and from all that I could then glean, and subsequently it is my firm conviction and belief that it was an enterprise created, or at least had its origin in Booth's own visionary mind, and totally disconnected with any person or persons in the service of the Confederate States government.

Booth's object was to undertake the abduction of Abraham Lincoln, convey him to Richmond, turn him over to the Confederate States government, to be held as a hostage for the exchange of prisoners, as the United States government had refused to exchange them. By doing so it would strengthen the force of the Confederate Army and be the means of filling up to some extent their depleted ranks. He pictured in most glowing terms how easy it could be accomplished.[6]

The Plans Outlined.

Often Abraham Lincoln, attended by no one except his carriage driver, visited the hospital over the Anacostia bridge. He [Booth] proposed to intercept him on one of these visits, take him, coachman and all, drive through the lower counties of Maryland, place him in a boat, cross the Potomac to Virginia and thence convey him to Richmond. Everything was prepared for this end, boat purchased and moored, to be moved at a moment's notice, and a boatman in waiting constantly at his bidding.

When the brain was to a great extent clouded by drink and reason, in a measure, had lost its power of concentrating thought, O'Laughlin and myself entered into the enterprise with Booth, after taking an oath to secrecy and good faith. The undertaking was for the sole purpose of bringing about an exchange of prisoners. The contemplated design within itself was purely humane and patriotic in its principles, void of all ambitions, aspirations or aggrandizement, and legitimate as an act of war.

There was no violence contemplated in the execution of the design other than the seizure of the body or person of Abraham Lincoln and his conveyance to Richmond, Va., as has already been set forth, as violence would have been in flat contradiction to his avowed purpose and the object to be attained. When I entered into the combination with him, my condition prevented me from giving it its proper consideration, otherwise I never would have been mixed up in the affair.

No Mercenary Incentive.

Men often do things upon the spur of the moment which they never would have done had they carefully looked and weighed the subject under discussion. Of course, had the attempt been made and we should have proved successful, or we had been taken or captured during its undertaking, the consequences attending it would have been of a very serious nature. There was no propelling force brought to bear, neither was assent to his proposition obtained under promise of pay or reward. No, it was the free outpouring of each heart, stripped of all mercenary motives or thought, which impelled the action of each.

The enterprise being deemed feasible and productive of good, we jointly entered into the plan as an act of honorable purpose, humanity and patriotism being the binding links to nerve us in the accomplishment of the design.

That was my first acquaintance with Michael O'Laughlin, and we three, Booth, O'Laughlin, and myself, comprised at that period the only persons engaged in the affair. The entire afternoon was spent in company with Booth, discussing measures to be adopted for the furtherance of his newborn enterprise. It was calculated to accomplish the undertaking before the coming election, in the month of November. Everything having been arranged satisfactorily, duties were apportioned for each to perform without delay and we parted company with one another, to meet again at a certain appointed time.

The Canadian Visit.

J. Wilkes Booth a few days later started for his home in the North, for the purpose of settling and arranging all his claims, etc., and to dispose of his property and possessions satisfactorily to himself, thence intending visiting Canada, ostensibly for the purpose of shipping his wardrobe by the way of Nassau to the Confederate States, purposing on his return from Canada the purchase of all required articles needed to carry out the enterprise.

At this point Mr. Arnold deals with the movements of Booth, of various conversations and with the purchase of the arms, etc. as detailed in the sworn statement taken before W.H. Gleason, the notary public, on December 3, 1867.[7] After detailing the change of plan to abduct Lincoln from the theater, because of his having ceased to visit the Soldiers' Home, Mr. Arnold writes:

Every preparation as far as known at this period had been completed, and each watched, as far as practicable, the movements of Lincoln, being cautious not to draw the attention, nor arouse the suspicions, of the numerous hordes of detectives and spies who at that time thronged every thoroughfare of the City of Washington. Mr. Lincoln during the month of January paid several visits to the theater, and had it been Booth's intention to have assassinated him at this time, he could have accomplished it with the same ease then that he did at a later period. In fact, many instances presented themselves, afar from the intercourse of a crowded city or a theater, when he could have done so, and perhaps none would have been able to have discovered whose hand it was that struck the blow.

Was a Monomaniac.

After detailing his first meeting with John H. Surratt,[8] Mr. Arnold says:

J. Wilkes Booth, if I may be allowed to pass an opinion, might have been justly termed a monomaniac on the subject. Each day he was becoming impressed more with the idea of attempting the abduction from the theater and nothing that could be advanced upon our part, tending to establish its utter impracticability, had the slightest weight or influence towards removing his erroneous impressions. It seemed to be his only thought by day and from his conversation, his frequent dreams by night.

Ambition, the curse of the world, was fast becoming the leading star in his destiny, destroying in its onward march the better feelings of his nature. Nervous irritability displayed itself on numerous occasions, in quick and short responses when information was asked: more especially so when combatting against his mode of procedure. From this time on his determination to carry out his plan of abduction at the theater grew stronger upon him daily, until it absorbed every other thought of his mind, and naught could be brought to bear to move or change him from his newly contemplated manner of carrying it out.

To me it seemed like the height of madness, and would but lead to the sacrifice of us all, without obtaining the object for which we combined together. The bravest heart, surrounded by foes, looks eagerly around for some opening of escape before he commences action. Thus it was with me, conscious of the fact that failure would be followed by arrest by the government of the United States, trial before a military tribunal on the specific charge of being spies, which would more than probably consign each to an ignominious death. All of this was brought to bear upon him, and conversed over, without producing the slightest effect in changing his resolve.

Opportunities Wasted.

On two occasions most favorable opportunities presented themselves, which, if Booth had energetically moved in the premises, or had a desire other than attempting it at the theater, I am perfectly confident that it would have proven successful beyond a doubt. These were occasions before I had become acquainted with the fact that others than Surratt and ourselves, already spoken of, were connected in the enterprise. The president passed over the Eastern Branch Bridge, accompanied only by his coachman, and a single guest within the carriage. To what point he went beyond was not known, his movements having been overlooked only so far as to ascertain the fact that he had passed over the river.[9]

Information was immediately conveyed to Booth of these occurrences. He paid but slight attention to the matter, on account, as he said, of the pressure of business at the time, and thus the only and most favorable opportunities were permitted to pass by without, it may be truly spoken, the slightest notice being taken there of him. It became impossible under these circumstances to feel like continuing in the affair, when inaction and inattention were becoming the ruling elements, delay tending to cause our positions daily to become more insecure.

The month of January had passed and as yet nothing had been accomplished. February ushered itself in, only to be a repetition of the former month; as Booth, through riotous living and dissipation, was compelled to visit the City of New York for the purpose of replenishing his squandered means. His absence continued nearly the entire month, caused by the great difficulty experienced in borrowing money. His visit did not extend beyond the City of New York, neither did he go for any other purpose than that above stated, which fact was made known to me on his return to Washington, on or about the 25th day of February, 1865.[10]

"Gas" Man Refused.

During my whole connection with Booth there was but one visit made to Canada by him, this occurring at or about the time of the St. Alban's raid, in which he was not concerned, his visit there being, as before stated, for the purpose of shipping his wardrobe by way of Nassau to the Confederate States.[11]

In his visit in New York in the month of February he tried to induce a man by the name of Samuel Knapp Chester to engage in the enterprise, he being, as Booth said, under obligations to him. The part allotted for him to perform was the turning off of the gas on the night in question, so that in the darkness enveloping the house and confusion created therefrom, the abduction could be made a success. Many things combining caused him to fail in this. Chester would take no part in it, and Booth determined to attempt it without the assistance of any others, other than those already connected with the affair.[12]

Chapter Seven
—

ARNOLD AND THE LINCOLN PLOT
—

Conspiracy to Capture the President
—

Idleness and Discontent---Plotters Spellbound by Booth---Booth's Plan a Quixotic Undertaking---Actor Makes Still Another Appeal---Had Booth But Returned to Acting---Two Detectives Arrive at Fortress Monroe---Other Names Mentioned by Detectives---Witnesses "Blinded by Gold"---Arnold Encounters a Confederate Prisoner---Has Reptiles for Bedfellows---Maintained Silence.

[Thursday, December 11, 1902]

During the entire month of February the project was at a standstill and I seldom met Booth.[1] For the first time my situation dawned upon me and began to be felt deeply. Here I was without any kind of employment, wandering from place to place in my idleness, making frequent visits to Baltimore, watched, no doubt, and my footsteps dogged by the government detectives and spies, who in various ways sought to obtain some clue as to my business and how engaged. This became insupportable, and as I felt every eye was watching my movements, thereby making my position very insecure.

After the presidential election[2] Booth worked energetically in the affair, and had completed all his arrangements, so he informed O'Laughlin and myself. He was always busy and in motion, having very limited time to hold conversation. I was unaware, even at this late date, that there were any others, beyond those spoken of before, who were connected with the affair.

Prisoners were now being exchanged and the purpose for which each had bound himself to the other and for which months of labor and time had been expended, had been accomplished.[3] Yet he still insisted upon carrying out the abduction. Patriotism had converged into heartless ambition on his part, and I looked upon him as a madman, and resolved, if the project were not speedily executed to sever my connection with him.[4]

Mr. Arnold next recites at length, as detailed in his sworn statement before Gleason, in 1867, of the meeting of the conspirators at Gotier's saloon and there meeting for the first time Lewis Payne, George A. Atzerodt and David E. Herold, who, with Arnold, Booth, O'Laughlin and Surratt, made up the party of conspirators that gathered in the private parlor of the saloon to discuss the abduction. Arnold says at this point that when Booth outlined the plans that his audience was seemingly carried away with his visionary ideas. Some few remarks of an objectionable character started a lengthy discussion. The fact that the suspicions of the government had seemingly been aroused from the fact that double stockades were being erected at the bridge crossing the Eastern Branch, on the Prince George's side of the river, which made the undertaking more difficult, even if success crowned the efforts at the theater, was talked over, and Arnold advanced the idea of the utter impracticability of the whole plan.[5]

Spellbound by Booth.

He then says: I stood not alone, yet none seemed to consider it in its proper light, they being completely spellbound by the utterances of Booth, not looking at the consequences which would follow. After arguing to great length, in fact until the subject became exhausted and before any reasonable decision could be arrived at or rendered, it culminated in a very exciting and violent controversy between Booth and myself, the others silently looking on when Booth, in his rashness and madness, finding that he could not swerve me from my purpose and firm stand taken in the manner of its accomplishment, threatened to shoot me, or words to that effect.

At this time it looked very much as if the meeting would be dissolved with serious consequences attending it, as two stubborn natures had met, and one of us decided a character as the other when deeming the position assumed as right. However, it was finally settled and compromised without resorting to shooting, after which, in the presence of the entire company, I stated my determination and firm resolve to sever my connection with the affair in case it was not carried out during the week, stating, also "Gentlemen, you have naught to fear from me in the matter, as I never would betray you."[6]

The resolve to attempt to carry off the president from the hospital or encampment on Seventh street, where the chief executive failed to appear after the conspirators had arrived on the scene on horseback, is dealt with again by Arnold at this point. The plan was to take the carriage of the President and all seated within it, drive it around by way of Bladensburg, thence through the lower counties in the direction of Port Tobacco, cross the river at or near that point, and thence onward to Richmond.

A Quixotic Undertaking.

Commenting on this plan, Mr. Arnold says: The most quixotic and visionary undertaking that ever entered a sane man's brain. I looked upon him as demented, but made no objection, stating that we would be ready at the appointed time. Of all the ideas existing in a man's brain, this was the most foolhardy ever advanced, and we concluded that it was done to try the nerve of his associates. We looked upon him as a madman, yet could offer no objection, from the fact that we had given our word to assist him in it during the week.

O'Laughlin, Payne and Arnold rode part of the way to the city in company, and Booth and Surratt went on out the road. What became of Atzerodt I am unable to state, and Herold was not present, he having been sent to T.B. or Surrattsville with Booth's horse and buggy, conveying the box containing the two carbines and other minor articles. About 8 o'clock that same evening O'Laughlin and myself met Booth and Surratt back of the National Hotel, at the stable where our horses had been placed at livery, and from that day I never saw John H. Surratt until I met him a clerk at the Norfolk Line of steamers in Baltimore, some 10 years ago.

The interval allotted for carrying out the scheme expired, and O'Laughlin and myself severed all connection with Booth and his confederates, and, in fact, the general idea of the entire party was that the project was entirely abandoned, and we returned to our respective homes in Baltimore on March 20, 1865.

Still Another Appeal.

But a few days had elapsed before Booth was again soliciting my assistance, to which I paid not the slightest attention. On March 25, 1865, as he returned from New York to the City of Washington he stopped in Baltimore, he called at my father's to see me, but I was in the country. So he left a letter for me, and I found that he desired to try it once more, and, if unsuccessful, to forever abandon it. As requested, I called at Barnum's Hotel, but found he had departed. I, therefore, concluded that he had gone to Washington, which caused the penning of the communication of March 27, which proved so fatal in its bearings in my respective case.

The motive of the letter was to prevent, if possible, his undertaking. Whether he left this letter in his trunk to betray me, in my innocence, into the hands of the government, through malice or forgetfulness I cannot fathom, nevertheless, it accomplished its end, and from this fact was forced to become a witness against myself.

The trip with O'Laughlin to Washington to get money from Booth, owing O'Laughlin, is dealt with at length.[7] He says: We had an interview with Booth at the National Hotel, and the scheme was entirely abandoned. During the conversation Booth informed us that he had learned through Lewis J. Weichman, with whom he was on the most friendly terms and from whom he derived all information relating to the number of prisoners held by the United States government, that John H. Surratt had accompanied a lady to Richmond, owing to the capture of the person by the United States authorities who had been in the habit of ferrying parties across the river, and it was through this circumstance alone that the services of Surratt were offered.[8]

Had He But Done So.

Among the last words uttered by Booth on that occasion were that he intended returning to his profession upon the stage and that he had given up forever his project. This was the last interview I ever had and the last time I ever met him, and I have never seen nor heard from him since. Of all the others connected with the affair I never saw nor heard from any after March 17, 1865, excepting Atzerodt, whom I accidentally ran upon March 31, on my visit to Washington.

After dealing with his securing work at Old Point Comfort; Mr. Arnold tells of the receipt of the news of Lincoln's assassination in the following words:

On the 15th of April, 1865, about 12 o'clock noon, whilst seated in the counting rooms at Mr. Wharton's at Old Point Comfort, Va., it became rumored that Abraham Lincoln had been assassinated the evening preceding, whilst walking along Pennsylvania Avenue, in Washington. The name of the person perpetrating the deed was unknown, in fact, the report was so vague that but few persons credited it. Towards evening, other dispatches arriving announced the assassination of Mr. Seward and other officials of the government. The greatest excitement prevailed.[9]

It was not until the following day that any clue had been obtained to the person who had committed the deed, when the public mind became gradually impressed with the idea that John W. Booth was the guilty hand that struck the blow. This news startled me, feeling assured that my former connection and intimacy with Booth would lead to my arrest, and to be even suspected I felt was almost equivalent to death.

Had I been differently situated, or been where I felt that the law would have protected me, I would have surrendered myself (in my entire innocence) into the hands of the government; but, as it was, I determined to let affairs pursue their own course, and quietly as possible, to my mind's excited condition, await my arrest.

Two Detectives Arrive.

On April 17, whilst seated in the store, two government detectives arrived and inquired for me. I went from the office and met them, when a letter was handed me by one of them, purporting to have been sent from my father, in which it was stated that a communication written to John Wilkes Booth, March 27, had been found within Booth's trunk, which seemed to connect me in some way with the deed committed and advising me to state all I knew concerning it.

After perusing it, the detectives asked whether I intended to comply with the request of my father. I stated yes, and told them that I knew nothing concerning it, nor was I at any time in any manner connected with Booth or others.[10] It became necessary from Booth's betrayal of me (no matter whether emanated from malice or forgetfulness) to become a witness against myself, and I was forced to acknowledge that I had been at one period in any unlawful undertaking.

I was then asked by the detectives if the communication found in Booth's trunk was written by me. I desired to be informed of some of its contents or expressions, where headed from and when dated. They gave me the desired information -- where dated from and how signed -- when, without hesitation or denial, I acknowledged it was penned by me. I did not deny writing it, as sworn by a witness on the stand; neither could it be expected that acknowledgement would be made to a communication before its contents were in a measure made known, as it was just as likely to have been written by someone else as myself.[11]

Other Names Mentioned.

The detectives were the first to mention the name of O'Laughlin, Surratt, and Atzerodt, and I was informed that

O'Laughlin had given himself up. Finding that suspicion had centered itself upon those with whom I had been associated, in conjunction with my betrayal by Booth, I deemed it necessary in justice not only to myself, but to those with whom I had been formerly connected, to state the whole truth, as embodied in the statement made on the 18th of April in Marshal McPhail's office, in Baltimore.[12]

After my acknowledgement to the foregoing facts I was taken into the back part of the storehouse, my person and baggage searched and property of a private nature confiscated, which to this day has never been returned, although I have repeatedly asked its restitution. There was nothing found of a compromising nature among my effects, because I had no correspondence with anyone during the time that I was employed by Mr. Wharton.[13]

I was then turned over to the military authorities, conveyed to a prison pen, where I remained during the best part of the day without a morsel of food and quizzed by some of the inmates, who seemed to be void of both reason and sense. In the afternoon I was brought before the provost marshal at Fortress Monroe, when I remained in the presence of its military dignitary for upwards of half an hour, and was thence conveyed to the steamboat, arriving in the City of Baltimore the next morning, and confined in the office of Provost Marshal McPhail, where I remained for the most part of the day.

Whilst there I was treated humanely, and the requirements of nature were fully provided. After sending for my father and seeing him, I made my written statement, requesting that I should make it in duplicate form so that he should be the possessor of a copy. The request was denied, why, can only be learned through the then secretary of war and the judge advocate general of the United States.

"Blinded by Gold."

`Tis a useless task I feel to attempt to controvert testimony adduced upon my trial, as emanating from verbal statements made by me, as witnesses were blinded by the amount of glittering gold, as their reward, large sums having been offered for the apprehension of anyone suspected of being connected with the crime. I pronounce the little that was adduced against me, through a detective, as false in its impressions and pervertive of truth, many words being transposed and others added, materially changing the whole tenor of its meaning.

But of this, at this time, I have naught to do. Let the

record of that infamous proceeding stand, in all its branches, with its false swearing, subordination of perjury, its hireling witnesses --- a towering monument of infamy, commemorating the corruptness and baseness of the hour. I deal alone with truth, acts of heartless inhumanity, cruelty and tyranny meted me by the government of the United States, before any charge as yet had been preferred or guilt (with all the base measures adopted to secure it) had been established in the case of any.

From the period of my arrest until April 18, 1865, whilst I was under the charge of and custody of Colonel Wooley,[14] my treatment was conducted upon principles of humanity and kindness. It was not until I was turned over to the custody of the commanding officer of Fort McHenry that harsh and cruel measures were resorted to, from orders no doubt emanating from Edwin M. Stanton, secretary of war.[15] I was placed in a loathsome and filthy cell, branded by suspicion as a felon, robbed of my liberty, resting under the grave charge of being implicated in the assassination of Abraham Lincoln.

A Confederate Prisoner.

This of itself was sufficient torture to one who possessed a sensitive nature, without the additional acts of inhumanity heaped upon me. There happened to be a Confederate prisoner of war occupying one of the small cells back of the one in which I was confined. I recognized his voice, we having been friends and companions from our earliest youth, and entered into conversation with him. This fact was reported [by] the sergeant of the guard to the officer of the day, and forthwith I was taken from my cell, brought before the one he occupied, carefully searched, this making some half dozen times in all, thence conveyed to the quarters of the commanding officer, who interrogated me to his heart's content, becoming as wise in the matter wherewith I was charged as I was myself, which seemed to displease him, if actions afterwards may be a criterion to judge by.

Calling his orderly, who was in attendance, I was committed to his charge, conducted to the guardhouse, stripped and thoroughly searched again. I was then thrown into a dungeon, beneath the earthwork of the fort, heavily ironed, hand and foot, where not a ray of light could penetrate, and left to muse with myself in total darkness, no place to lie but the damp, slimy floor, void of covering of any description beneath or above. Looking upon the rough visage of my guardian or jailer as the door opened, I attempted to read his heart by the expression of his face, but found as callous and as cold as the other, from which but little could be expected.

He was a soldier every inch. I requested a blanket be furnished me, to keep myself warm, which request was unexpectedly complied with in the course of half an hour or so. The massive doors of iron creaked on their rusty hinges, as it was again closed, shutting out every ray of light, leaving a feeling like unto one buried in a grave. Food soon after, in the shape of bread and coffee, was brought, as reported by the sergeant, it being impossible to penetrate the darkness, and I was then left alone, a sentinel, like unto a bronze statue, keeping guard before my iron-doored cell.

Reptiles for Bedfellows.

Covering my person, head and foot, to prevent rats and poisonous reptiles from coming in contact with my body, I soon was wrapped in sleep, out of which, at midnight, I was rudely aroused, brought again to the guardhouse and ordered to dress myself in quick haste. Surprised at such movements and utterly confounded, I attempted to fathom the surroundings, as to these mysterious actions. I thought the days of the French Revolution, with its hideous and barbaric murders, were going to be re-enacted in the republic, and that I was thus taken out to be either shot or hung. Callous and indifferent to my fate, with my usual haste, I dressed myself as instructed.

As soon as I was in readiness an ambulance was driven up to the door of the guardhouse, and I was placed within it, weighted down with heavy irons and, with an armed escort, was driven to the Camden Street Depot, where I was turned over again to Marshal McPhail and his accompanying detectives, who transferred me (after the weighty irons had been removed and those of lighter material placed upon my wrists) to a special car in attendance, whence I was transported to Washington.

Maintained Silence.

During my trip there my lips were sealed to those by whom I was surrounded, I being determined not to let them manufacture testimony against me. On arrival in Washington I was placed in a hack and driven to the navy yard, where I was in the hands of the United States government. They confined me in a narrow and limited apartment, used as a closet, aboard an iron-clad monitor, and irons of torturous manufacture were placed upon my wrists, and I had nothing but the hard, uneven surface of the closet to lie upon.[16]

The irons were so tightly fitted that the blood could not

circulate, and my hands became fearfully swollen, the outward skin changing its appearance to a mixture of black, red and purple color. This fact was reported to Captain Munroe,[17] who kindly had them changed and a pair that fitted easier placed upon me. The heat was intense. The atmosphere breathed was obtained through a register, as it was puffed up by fans used for this purpose. It more frequently happened than otherwise that the machine was not at work, which caused a suffocating sensation to creep over me. To sleep was an impossibility on account of the extreme pain accruing from the torturous irons used.

Chapter Eight

—

THE CONSPIRACY TRIAL

—

Judgment of the Military Court

—

Cruelty on Board the Monitor---Thought Life Was Short---Arnold Confined at Arsenal---The Military Court---Prisoners Hooded and Ironed---Secret Conversations in the Prison Yard---Mysterious Sounds of Hammering---Four Meet Their Doom---The Lincoln Assassination Avenged---Chains Caused Torture---Prisoners Informed of Ship's Destination.

[Friday, December 12, 1902]

For several days my condition remained unchanged. Two sentinels closely guarded the entrance to my quarters, who, in every instance, were kind. Finding my frame becoming reduced and the great pains attached to lying so long on hard boards, I made a request of the officer of the day to furnish me something to lie upon, which was complied with, but only that other acts of heartless cruelty and inhumanity should follow. A few days afterwards, or about the 25th of April, Captain Munroe, United States Marines, under whose charge I was, came into my quarters and in a very soft and kind voice stated that he had orders from Edwin M. Stanton, secretary of war, to encase my head in a cap, that I must not become alarmed and that it would remain but a few days, at the same time ordering shackles to be placed upon my ankles.[1]

But a few hours passed when the orders were carried into execution by the officer of the day. The covering for the head was made of canvas, which covered the entire head and face, dropping down in front to the lower portion of the chest. It had cords attached, which were tied around the neck and body in such manner that to remove it was a physical impossibility. No doubt Stanton wished to accustom me to the death cap before execution.

During my stay upon the monitor these particular acts of cruelty and inhumanity were continued, it being with the greatest difficulty, and frequently impossible, to place food in my mouth, a sentinel kindly volunteering his services to perform that office for me. This continued about a week, as far as I could judge, during which period daylight never lit upon the eye, they not even permitting the cap to be withdrawn for the purpose of washing the swollen, bloated and soiled visage.

The mystery which attended each movement from the period that the United States authorities took possession of me was again brought more heavily into requisition, and I was removed through orders received through the War Department from the monitor at the usual hour set apart -- midnight. As the silent hour drew near, the dragging and clanking of chains was heard overhead, as victim after victim passed to and fro to the place provided for his reception, and then all became silent as death again.[2]

Thought Life Was Short.

From torture already inflicted upon me I deemed that my span of life was quickly drawing to a close and that those who had preceded me, from the deep silence reigning, had been consigned to a watery grave. I awaited silently the supposed approaching hour of my doom, convinced that a man who could resort to such inhumanity to his fellow-man as had already been practiced in my case had soul enough for other things. I was soon aroused from this train of thought, which was of anything but a pleasant nature, by the officer of the guard, who ordered me to hold myself in readiness for removal.

Within a very limited time afterwards I felt the tight grasp of some human hand upon each arm, as I was hurriedly and roughly conveyed from my quarters to the deck of the monitor, where I was hustled here and there by those who supported me on either side. It was impossible to learn where I was being conducted, as my head was still muffled in the bag, drawn tight around my head and throat almost to suffocation. However, I soon became aware from the spring and bend beneath my footsteps that I was being conducted upon the gangplank to some other vessel, and in a few moments I was thrust upon a bench upon its deck and strictly commanded to silence.

All the details attending this midnight mockery of justice being completed, the whistle was blown, and, from the movements and noise, I found I was aboard some sidewheeled steamer.[3] It seemed like hours before she started on her trip, first moving ahead and then backing repeatedly, until finally, having assumed the right position, she quickly sped on her way, landing me finally at some unknown point, where I was compelled to walk a long distance, through mud and water, with irons on my ankles eating deep into the flesh, and the rough handling of my arms by those who had me in charge, bruising and otherwise lacerating my wrists by the torturous irons used.

Confined at Arsenal.

Arriving at my final destination (the Arsenal as I afterwards learned) I was conducted up and down long flights of stairs and finally thrust into a damp and narrow cell upon the ground floor of the building.[4] Bed and blanket were supplied here. The next morning I was given a cup of coffee and a very small slice of bread. This was the only food issued until the following day.[5] I could hear the warblings of the birds around about and occasionally the crowing of a cock, and, as forts and bastiles had been to date the order of proceedings, I judged I had at last found a home in a dungeon at Fort Washington.[6]

It was a relief to think that I had at last arrived at my final destination or resting place, as every movement so far had been attended in each instance with increased pain and suffering. The canvas bag still continued upon my head, I never having been allowed its removal to wash my swollen face. I had been but a few days incarcerated at this place when I was aroused at midnight in my cell by Major General Hartranft, holding in his hand a lantern and some papers, which I saw after the removal of the hood from my head.

He asked me if I could read, to which I replied in the affirmative. He then placed in my hand a paper containing the charge and specifications against me and others, which I perused in that silent midnight hour by the dim glimmer of a lantern, after which (the hood being replaced upon my head) he retired, leaving me to ponder over the charge alone in my cell.

The next morning I was removed from my cell and conveyed up several flights of stairs, to be seated upon a bench, when the hood was removed and I found myself in the presence of a number of the martial heroes of the United States, decked in their glittering uniforms, and on either side, victims like unto myself, weighted down with chains and irons.

The Military Court.

The court of military inquisition was convened, the charge read to each by Assistant Judge Advocate Bingham,[7] who asked if we had any objection to any member of the court. As it was useless to object, each replied in the negative. I pleaded "not guilty" to the charge. After the pleading of each of those arraigned was over, the hoods were placed upon our heads as formerly before removal from court, and I was removed amidst the clanking of irons again to my cell to wait there until the next morning.

The next day I was taken from my cell, my clothing and the hood removed, and I was ordered to bathe myself. I cannot conceive how I escaped from receiving my death, as the water used was as cold as ice itself, it having been taken from the barrels used for making ice-water. My whole frame shook and trembled from contact with this cold fluid, until my limbs nearly shook from beneath my body.

A detective, seeing me shivering and trembling in such a manner, inquired what ailed me, if I were ill, etc., when he knew within his own vile heart the causes of my suffering. After the bath a change of clean clothing was furnished. I was taken back to my cell, when I found that a differently constructed hood had been prepared for a head cover of a much more torturous and painful pattern than the one formerly used.[8]

It fitted the head tightly, containing cotton pads, which were placed directly over the eyes and ears, having the tendency to push the eyeballs far back in the sockets. One small aperture allowed about the nose through which to breathe, and one by which food could be served to the mouth, thence extending with lap ears on either side to the chin, to which were attached eyelets and cords, the same extending also from the crown of the head backwards to the neck. The cords were drawn as tight as the jailor in charge could pull them, causing the most excruciating pain and suffering, and then tied in such a manner around the neck that it was impossible to remove them.

Hooded and Ironed.

Thus hooded and doubly ironed I remained day after day, until months had circled themselves away, condemned unheard, crime imputed and branded as guilty before guilt had been established even by that inquisition court, a military commission, before which I was afterwards tried in mockery. This manner of treatment continued uninterrupted, the hoods never being removed except when I was brought before the court and always replaced on exit, if but a moment intervened, from on or about April 25 to June 10, 1865.

The surgeon in charge expressed his opinion that the hoods had the same effect upon the head and brain as if it had been encased in a poultice. These inflictions of punishment and torture were practiced upon nearly all of the others. They have all passed to the bar of God, suffering on earth ended, and silently awaiting justice at the hands of the Almighty, in whose presence truth shall be revealed. Man can hide it from his fellow-man, but the truth will be established before the bar of God.[9]

This was the justice meted to me before trial. What could be expected when the trial itself took place. During the period of our suffering Atzerodt was daily taken from his cell into the outer prison yard, his irons and hood removed, accompanied by detectives and hireling spies, holding out to him hope of life in case he divulged all the particulars and knowledge he possessed relative to the parties connected with the assassination. That he informed them of each and every particular is not to be doubted, and with all these infamous proceedings by detectives, courts inside and inquisitions outside, failure stamped itself in connecting me in the assassination of Abraham Lincoln, as the decision of that drumhead court-martial proved the truth of the statement made in Marshal McPhail's office after my arrest.[10]

Secret Conversations.

After June 10[11] I, with others, was permitted two hours recreation and exercise in the outer yard attached to the prison, where frequently, unobserved, I held converse in broken expressions with Herold, Payne, and Atzerodt. We were not permitted to speak, it is true, being strictly and closely guarded by armed sentinels, overlooked by the officers of the prison. David E. Herold, in the presence of Colonel McCall, Major Frederick Herbert and the government detectives, stated that John H. Surratt was not in the City of Washington at the time of the assassination, nor had he been seen by Booth since his visit to Richmond, on March 23, 1865.[12]

Herold and Payne also publicly expressed that Mrs. Surratt was an innocent woman, which was reiterated by Payne in the presence of his executors [*sic*], as he ascended to the fatal trap which launched his soul into eternity.

We were permitted this outside recreation from June 10 until our departure from there on July 17, 1865. Irons were removed on these occasions, but immediately replaced upon my return to my cell. Bibles presented by some humane heart during the trial of some of the prisoners were taken from them by the officer in charge, they not being permitted to gain consolation even from God's holy writings. Nor were they ever furnished through their own good will, I myself having made the request to be permitted to apply to my father to furnish me a Testament. General Hartranft stated he would obtain them from the Christian Association and deliver them to us. They were furnished, as well as memory can recall, about 2 o'clock on the afternoon before the execution took place, as we were returning to our cells from the prison yard.[13]

Mysterious Sounds.

That same afternoon the noise of hammers was distinctly heard, as if some repairing about the building was being done. I tried to concentrate my thoughts in an attempt to unravel its meaning, never for an instant dreaming that they were erecting the scaffold to launch human souls into endless eternity in such quick and sudden haste. The hammerings continued throughout the afternoon until late, when the noise from the hammers ceased. The next morning there was an unusual movement of feet hurrying to and fro, the rattling of chains and dragging of ponderous balls on the brick pavement in front of my cell.

I could not surmise the cause for all these mysterious movements, and finally concluded that fresh victims were being brought. Knowing the utter impossibility to obtain information relative to those proceedings, or what it could mean, I became composed, as far as composure was possible, and amused myself, as heretofore, in counting the number of small squares visible in the iron door of my cell, the number of layers of brick in the floor, the heighth of the ceiling of my cell, the flies and insects, which had come to share my narrow and cheerless domain.

About 2 o'clock in the afternoon General Dodd came to my cell, seating himself upon a small box, which had lately been granted me for use as a table, and asked if I had noticed anything of an unusual nature pervading the prison. I replied in the affirmative, giving him an account of the bustle and confusion, attended with the clanking of irons, etc., throughout the morning, and that I judged from these circumstances that other prisoners had arrived.

Four Meet Their Doom.

He replied no, and in a soft and feeling manner informed me of the execution of four of our number.[14] I was completely thunderstruck and amazed, and felt within my own heart, from expressions gained from Herold and Payne during our joint incarceration, that a fearful crime had been perpetrated by the United States government in the execution of an innocent woman. That feeling has been verified and her innocence has been publicly proclaimed by thousands of the leading men, not only of this, but of other nations.

A few days after the execution we were again allowed exercise in the outer yard of the prison, which on entering forced us to be confronted by that huge machine of death, and a little to the south side of it the eye rested upon four mounds of new heaped earth, testifying the undeniable fact that beneath those cold and cheerless hillocks rested in the quiet sleep of death all that but a few days before were life and sensibility. Day after day we confronted this scene, the scaffold remaining in all its hideousness, involuntarily causing the eye to wander and gaze upon the small mounds, marking its feast of death.

The Execution: Mrs. Surratt, Powell, Herold and Atzerodt

Every day we passed through these evolutions, all anxiety to learn what decision the court had arrived at in our own respective cases. On the afternoon of July 17 we were summoned separately to the presence of General Hartranft, the military custodian, who was seated at the farther end of the yard, and the sentence of each was made known, as found by the military commission, failing, however, to disclose the fact, and concealing from each the sentence as modified by Andrew Johnson, President of the United States.[15]

Assassination Avenged.

The military commission had fulfilled its mission: the death of Abraham Lincoln had been avenged, the public cry for vengeance had been appeased, and the long drawn out trial, which for two months had heaped fuel to the fire to add to the public excitement, passed out of existence and the nation at large became pacified.

The midnight hour, which had been set apart for removal

in every instance, was again resorted to, and we were silently marched, double-ironed, to a steamboat lying in the Potomac moored at a wharf. Each side of the wharf was lined with armed sentinels and soldiers, as we emerged from our prison gates, and as we passed between them on the way to the boat our clanking irons in the solemn midnight seeming to pierce the vaults of heaven, crying out to the living God for vengeance on those who had traduced, defamed and victimized us, to satiate the public cry for revenge.

On arrival on board the steamer which was in waiting to receive us we were swiftly conveyed down the river, to what destination was unknown. On the afternoon of July 18 we arrived at Fortress Monroe, when we were transferred from the steamer to a small tugboat, thence, under heavy guard, to the gunboat *Florida*, Captain Budd[16] commanding. The irons had been removed temporarily from our wrists, and shackled about our feet we were compelled to ascend the ladder to the deck of the gunboat, where the entire crew of seamen stood about gazing in mute wonder. On landing upon the deck of the gunboat, Capt. William H. [*sic*] Dutton,[17] in charge of the guard, directed that the Lilly irons be replaced upon our wrists. They had been placed upon Spangler and I, when the order of Captain Dutton was countermanded by General Dodd, and the irons were removed.

Chains Caused Torture.

No sooner were we upon the gunboat than we were ordered into the lower hold of the vessel. It required, in our shackled condition, the greatest care to safely reach there, owing to the limited space, eight inches of chain being allowed between our ankles. After leaving the second deck we were forced to descend upon a ladder whose rounds were distant so far apart that the chains bruised and lacerated the flesh and even the bone of the ankles. We remained in the sweltering hole during the night in an atmosphere pregnant with disagreeable odors, arising from various articles of subsistence stored within, and about 8 o'clock next morning we passed through another ordeal in our ascent to the deck, which was attended with more pain than the descent, owing to the raw condition of our wounds.[18]

All intercourse with the crew was prohibited, guards being stationed around us, and we were not permitted to move without being accompanied by an armed marine. Subsistence of the grossest kind was issued, in the shape of fat salt pork and hard-tack. We remained on deck during the day, closely watching, as far as we were able, the steering of the vessel by the sun, and found we were steaming due South. The course was unchanged the next day and I began to suspect that fatal isle, the Dry Tortugas, was our destined home of the future.

Informed of Destination.

From this time out we remained on deck, our beds being brought up at night and taken between decks in the morning. Arriving off Hilton Head, S.C., and whilst lying in port, we were informed by General Dodd that he was sailing under sealed orders, but as soon as we left the port he would announce our destination. We remained there during the night, having received some guests on board, and the officers amused themselves with dancing and carousing. About 12 o'clock in the day we were informed that the Dry Tortugas was our destination.

Of it I had no idea beyond that gathered through the columns of the press, in which it had been depicted as a perfect hell, which fact was duly established by imprisonment on its limited space. After the second day on the ocean the irons were removed from our feet during the day, but replaced at night, and we were permitted from this day out the privilege of being on deck on account of the oppressive heat of the climate, where we could catch the cool sea breeze as it swept across the deck in the ship's onward track over the bounding ocean.

Chapter Nine

—

"LEAVETH ALL HOPE BEHIND"

—

Life in the Dry Tortugas

—

Arrival at the Fort---Spangler a Handy Man---Many Federal Prisoners---
"Conspirators" Placed in a Casemate---Colonel Grenfell Arrives---Alleged Plan
to Rescue Prisoners---Official Communications on Rescue Plot---Copy of
Stanton's Telegram---Dr. Mudd's Position in the Hospital---Place Leaders of
Plot in Irons.

[Saturday, December 13, 1902]

We arrived in sight of Fort Jefferson, Dry Tortugas, Fla., on July 24, 1865. When nearing the grim-looking walls, a signal gun was fired from the gunboat, which was responded to by the officer in command of the fort, and soon the officer of the day made his appearance on board, and was informed of the object of the visit of the boat, etc. Within a very short time we were placed within a small boat, were conveyed to the fort, and placed within one of the many casemates existing there.

The officers who had had us in charge remained at the fort a sufficient length of time to have, as it is called, a lark. After three months of torture both of body and mind, we thought that we had at last found a haven of rest, although in a government Bastile, where, shut out from the world, we would dwell and pass the remaining days of our life. It was a sad thought, yet it had to be borne.

We were now left under the charge of Col. Charles Hamilton, One Hundred and Tenth New York Volunteers, who was at that period commandant of the post. He gave us instructions relative to the rules in force, stating the consequences which would attend any breach in discipline, finally impressing upon our minds that there was a dark and gloomy dungeon within the fort, to which offenders against the rules were consigned, over whose entrances was inscribed the classic words: "Whoso entereth here leaveth all hope behind."

We asked him if there were any special instructions relating to us, to which he replied: "No, you have the same privilege of the island as any person confined here, no instructions to the contrary having been furnished by the War Department in your cases." Our bed that night was constituted of "a soft plank," and, in fact, so continued for months, until, through our own exertions and means received from home, we were able to purchase pieces of canvas, wherewith to nail up a rudely constructed bed.

Spangler a Handy Man.

Spangler's trade was a godsend at this time, and proved so on more than one occasion afterwards. The next morning we walked around the enclosure of the fort and towards evening strolled around the breakwater wall for the purpose of forming some idea of our desolate condition. The Dry Tortugas is a small island isolated in the Gulf of Mexico in about 25 degrees north of the equator, comprising in all seven and a half acres of land, and lying directly beneath the rays of a tropical sun. It is located 65 miles north west from Key West, 95 miles north from Cuba and about 200 miles directly south from Tampa, Fla., this being the nearest connecting point with the mainlands of Florida.

Fort Jefferson

Upon its limited area was erected a huge and massive structure, hexagon shaped, of brick and mortar, in an unfinished condition, called Fort Jefferson. When completed, if ever, it would mount 480 guns. On the outer side of the fort there existed a wide and deep moat, to prevent the surging of the sea from washing against the main structure itself, and intended at the same time as a defense against assaulting columns. It is ocean girt on either side, strongly protected by coral reefs and intricate channels on approach.[1]

On our arrival the island was entirely destitute of vegetable matter, with the exception of some few bushes of small growth, and a dozen cocoanut trees, which had been planted many years back by the hand of man. Beyond this there was naught to gaze upon inside save the white, glittering coral sand, which had a very injurious effect upon the eyes in many cases, causing men to become totally blind after dark, a disease known there and of frequent occurrence, termed moon-blind.

Many Federal Prisoners.

There were upward of 600 federal prisoners confined there for various offenses against military rules and laws, who were compelled to labor daily, from morn till night, upon limited and loathsome sustenance. Without exception, it was the most horrible place the eye of man ever rested upon, where day after day the miserable existence was being dragged out, intermixed with sickness, bodily suffering, want and pinching hunger, without the additional acts of torture and inhumanity that soon I became a witness of.[2]

Around about the fort there were several small keys, termed, respectively, Sand, East, Bird and Loggerhead Keys. Sand Key, very small in area, lies in a northeasterly direction, distant about half a mile, upon which had been erected a hospital for quarantine purposes and to be used in case of any epidemic occurring at the fort. Every foot of its space is now peopled with the dead, many of the bodies having been washed up by the surf of the sea, and the hospital building having been torn down for the purpose of erecting a theater at the post.

Bird Key, the largest in area, is distant about five miles from the Dry Tortugas, upon which, in the summer season, sea gulls in dense flocks congregate to deposit their eggs. These were gathered by the garrison and used for food. East Key lies in a southwesterly direction, distant about one mile from the fort, and was used as a cemetery for the dead. Loggerhead Key lies northerly, about three and one-half miles from the fort, upon which is erected a lighthouse of great height, used as a guide to ships to prevent their running upon the reefy beds which abound.

Those were all the points of land visible, all else was the deep and briny ocean. I looked long and intently upon all the surroundings of the place, and asked the question: "Is this, indeed, to be my home for life?"

Placed in a Casemate.

When we had returned from our walk around the breakwater wall we were placed within our dingy casemate for the night. Food issued was horrible in the extreme. Many were suffering dreadfully from scurvy and chronic troubles. The bread was disgusting to look upon, being a mixture of flour, bugs, sticks and dirt. Meat, whose taint could be traced by its smell from one part of the fort to the other; in fact, rotten, and to such an extent that dogs ran from coming in contact with it, was served. No vegetable diet was issued of any description, and the coffee, which should have been good, as good quality was issued, was made into a slop by those who had charge of the cookhouse. These articles, with but little variation, composed the diet until the Fifth United States Artillery arrived and assumed command, which was in the month of November.

Up to the above date there was not an article of food raised upon the island. The meat and flour that had been repeatedly condemned by the inspector, the quartermaster still issued, not only to prisoners, but, in many instances, to the garrison. Our treatment during the stay of Colonel Hamilton, of the One Hundred and Tenth New York Volunteers was as good as could be expected under such circumstances.

In a short time the One Hundred and Tenth New York was relieved by the One Hundred and Sixty-first New York, under whom we received far better treatment, no change occurring, however, in the nature and kind of food issued, it still being of the meanest and coarsest nature. The stay of this regiment was very short, and they were relieved by the Eighty-second United States Colored Infantry, under whom the first change occurred, rendering imprisonment almost insupportable.

Dr. Samuel Mudd, upon the arrival of the Eighty-second Regiment, on September 25, 1865, made an attempt to escape, because, as he afterward informed me, he was fearful that his life would be sacrificed under their rule.[3] Under the plea of the attempt of Mudd to escape, each of us was placed within a dungeon and shackles were placed around our ankles, and in this degraded condition we were compelled to daily perform certain assigned labor.

Colonel Grenfell Arrives.

Col. George St. Leger Grenfell, quite an aged gentleman,

arrived at the fort shortly after Mudd's attempt at escape, under the alleged charge of conspiracy, and was placed in the same dungeon with us, and the same shameful indignity and degradation heaped upon him,[4] which leads me to suppose that Dr. Mudd's attempt at escape was not the true grounds, upon which this act of barbarity and inhumanity was based.[5] It was hardly known throughout the country as yet that we had been sent to Dry Tortugas. The War Department, under whose sealed orders we were sent to Dry Tortugas, knew of the fact of our arrival, and so did its chief detective, Gen. L.C. Baker, who must have started on his tour of the western part of the country about the same period as our departure from Washington, from the fact that less than a month had passed away before he had unearthed another conspiracy, which was organizing to rescue our imprisoned bodies from the authorities at Dry Tortugas.

The country seemed to be infested with conspiracies, or, at least, the heads of the different departments of the government breathed only poisonous vapors of combinations of persons combining together in some unlawful enterprise. Why was this so? I will answer it in a very few words. They were the conspirators themselves, conspiring not only against the innocent citizens of the republic, but against the republic itself, creating a necessity for the purpose of carrying out the natural propensity of their own hearts. To cover up their own natures in the transaction they stooped to deception and caused to be stated that the reason for placing us in irons, etc., was Mudd's attempt at escape.

Alleged Rescue Plan.

That it was all false and was so from the beginning I will endeavor to prove, using their own weapons, as will be seen by the following copy of a telegram, which was forwarded to the commanding officer of the Dry Tortugas, for his guidance and instruction; viz.:

Louisville, Ky.
August 17, 1865., 9 A.M.

Hon. T.T. Echart, Acting Assistant Secretary of War:

I have important papers. I think the commanding officer of Dry Tortugas should be put on guard against an attempt to rescue the state prisoners in his charge. A company is organizing in New Orleans for that purpose. I have all the facts from a reliable source.

(Signed)   L.C. BAKER[6]
...... Brig. Gen. Pro. Mar., War Dep't.

A true copy.
A. Gen'l's Office, August 17, 1865.

(Signed)   E.D. TOWNSEND
Asst. Adjt. Gen'l.

News of this conspiracy organizing, not organized, was communicated to each department commander, and soon all were in wild commotion, each endeavoring to outdo the other in their attempt to render abortive the object of that which had no existence beyond their own designing minds.

Official Communications.

In quick succession communications from the different headquarters arrived at the post, copies of which I herewith append.

War Dep't., A.Gen'l's Office.
Washington, August 17, 1865.

Col. C.H. Hamilton, 110 N.Y. Vol., or
The Commanding Officer, Dry Tortugas, Fla.

Sir: I enclose herewith a copy of a telegram from Brigadier General L.C. Baker, provost marshal of the War Department. The Secretary of War directs that besides taking effectual measures against any attempt to rescue prisoners you will place the four state prisoners -- Arnold, Mudd, Spangler and O'Laughlin -- under such restraint and within such limits inside Fort Jefferson as shall make abortive any attempt at escape or rescue. You will return by Lieutenant Carpenter, the bearer of this, a full report of the measures you take under these instructions.

Very respectfully,
Your obedient servant,

(Signed)   E.D. TOWNSEND
Assistant Adjutant General.

Headquarters Division of the Gulf,
New Orleans, August 20, 1865.

Commanding Officer, Tortugas:
The enclosed telegram is forwarded for your information.
You will at once take measures to prevent the accomplishment
of such purpose as the surprise of your post and the release of
the prisoners there. Report by return of the bearer the strength
of your garrison.

Very respectfully,
Your obedient servant,

(Signed)   P.H. SHERIDAN,
Major General.

Copy of Telegram.

Washington, August 17, 12:30 P.M.

Major General E.R.S. Canby:
This department is informed that an operation is on foot
in New Orleans to go to the Dry Tortugas and by surprise or
stratagem seize that place and release the prisoners there.
Immediately receiving this telegram, please send a special
messenger to notify the commander at Key West and Dry
Tortugas to take strict measures to guard against any stratagem
or surprise, and secure the safety of their commands. You will
also notify the division commander and request his co-opera-
tion. Acknowledge the receipt of this telegram.

(Signed)   E.M. STANTON
Secretary of War

Official.

(Signed)   P.H. SHERIDAN,
Major General.

As instructed, Lieutenant Carpenter, bearing these
dispatches, arrived at Fort Jefferson, Fla. during the month of
September, whilst Major Willis E. Craig, One Hundred and
Sixty-first N.Y. Volunteers, was in command. Captain Prentiss,
provost marshal in charge, forwarded the required information
relative to the strength of the garrison and the measures
adopted in our method of confinement, which seemed to be

satisfactory, as we were not molested nor restricted in any particular in the privileges thus far granted, and things went on as usual until September 25, the day the One Hundred and Sixty-first N.Y. Volunteers were relieved by the Eighty-second United States Colored Infantry, Major George E. Wentworth commanding, the period of Dr. Mudd's attempt to escape.

Dr. Mudd's Position.

Dr. Mudd occupied quarters at the post hospital building, where he had been given the position of ward master. We never met except at morning and at night, going and returning from work. I was perfectly ignorant that he entertained the idea of attempting escape. His secret was kept entirely within himself. At the time I was confined to my bed with a very severe case of break-bone fever, when the news reached me of Dr. Mudd's attempt to escape, and I was informed by Captain Prentiss that he thought that it would have an injurious effect upon each of us, as each would be held responsible for the acts of the other.

Dr. Samuel A. Mudd

Strict post orders were forthwith issued in Dr. Mudd's case, and he was ironed and placed within one of the cells attached to the guardhouse, and compelled during the day to perform the most menial labor on the island.[7] In fact, they could not hunt up hard enough work with which to vent their spleen upon him. It was legitimately his place to escape from his imprisonment if he could, and it was the place of his jailers to prevent it if possible, without resorting to such cruelties as were afterwards imposed upon us. Soon the seed of persecution became engrafted, from which each was to bear like part. It could be read upon the countenance of every officer, and rumors gradually ripened into facts.

Major General Foster,[8] commanding the Department of Florida, arrived upon the island, verbally left instructions with the commanding officer, and I was removed from the office of the provost marshal, where I had been employed soon after I landed at the fort, under the plea that these positions should alone be given to men in their own army or service capable of fulfilling the required duties thereof.

Place Leaders in Irons.

In a very short time thereafter the following communication was received at the post:

> Headquarters of Middle Florida.
> Second Separate Brigade, D.T.
> Tallahassee, September 3, 1865.

To the Commanding Officer, Sub.District, Key West:
Sir: Official information has been received at these headquarters from Washington that a plot exists to release the prisoners at Fort Jefferson. You will take the proper precautions to prevent any uprising of the prisoners, and, in case you find this information to be correct, take measures to ferret out the leaders and place them in irons.

By command of Brigadier General Newton.

(Signed) A.C. PROTZ
First Lieutenant and A.A. General.

Copy furnished.
Commanding Officer Dry Tortugas.

By referring to the previous communication it will be seen that in the first instance L.C. Baker obtained the facts from a reliable source that a conspiracy was organized in New Orleans to release the state prisoners confined at Fort Jefferson, Fla. This information was gained by him on August 17, 1865, and immediately telegraphed to the War Department at Washington. In less than a month, commands and telegrams having been forwarded here and there, finally culminated in establishing the conspiracy, as seen by communications from General Newton,[9] as existing at Dry Tortugas itself, he ordering, if it be found correct, that the leaders be placed in irons.

Therefore, no such conspiracy as detailed by General Baker ever existed, excepting in his own inventive mind. We were made the leaders so that further persecution and tortures could be heaped upon us. The finding of the court was insufficient, tortures already inflicted were not enough to satisfy the pent-up hatred of those in high positions against us, their defamed and traduced victims of military injustice.

Chapter Ten

—

A PRISONER OF STATE

—

Beneath Liberty's Banner

—

*Life In the Dungeon---Amid Mazy Windings---O'Laughlin's Useless Protest---
Again Put In Irons---Arnold Employed as Clerk---State Prisoners Together
Once More---Dungeon Was Flooding---Rain Water Bailed Out---Prisoners Fell
Within Their Tracks---Relief for Colonel Grenfell.*

[Sunday, December 14, 1902]

In a short time a damp and unhealthy dungeon was placed in readiness to receive us, through which but little air could penetrate, and on October 18, Col. G. St. Leger Grenfell, Mudd, Spangler, O'Laughlin and myself were removed to these selected quarters and herded together like so many cattle. The doors for the first few days were closed, with an armed sentinel walking to and fro from his seat, closely guarding against any approach to our quarters.

Soon leg irons were introduced, and each ironed, with the exception of myself, they remaining off me, because I was engaged in writing for some of the officers at post headquarters. When the instructions contained in General Newton's communication of September 3 had been looked into, the ringleaders of the plot ferreted out and placed in irons, the commanding officer, to prove how willingly the duty of his superior, but likewise of himself, had been performed, penned the following communication to the War Department:[1]

Headquarters, Fort Jefferson, Fla.
October 20, 1865.

Brevet Lieut. Col. Samuel Breck,
Assistant Adjutant General:

Colonel -- I have the honor to report that when I relieved Major Willis E. Craig, One Hundred and Sixty-first New York Volunteers, of the command of this post, he failed to turn over to me any particular order or instructions relative to the confinement of state prisoners at this post, and today for the first time, learned from Brigadier General Newton, commanding Department of Middle Florida, that instructions had been sent to the commanding officer of this post to keep them in close confinement, when not at work. When this post was visited by Major General Foster, commanding Department of Florida, on the 14th day of this month, he gave me instructions to put them in close confinement, and I have accordingly fitted up a dungeon to carry out his instructions, but I had never until this day known anything in regard to the orders from the War Department.

I am, sir,

Very respectfully,
Your obedient servant,
(Signed)   GEO. E. WENTWORTH
Major, Eighty-second United States Colored Infantry, commanding.

Amid Mazy Windings.

What mind amongst those mazy windings can unearth the cause of all these secret machinations. Everything connected so far as to the cause assigned for the placing of us in irons has been refuted by their own correspondence. We were closely confined, when not at work, in this damp and ill-ventilated dungeon, prepared by Major George E. Wentworth, for our reception --- forced to labor daily, heavily ironed about our feet, our footsteps closely followed by an armed guard (black), denied intercourse with everyone upon the island and locked within our gloomy dungeon at sundown.

Interior of Ft. Jefferson; conspirator cell in center

This continued unchanged until the arrival of the Fifth Artillery, Brigadier General Bennett H. Hill, commanding. The rations issued at this time were putrid, unfit to eat, and during these three months of confinement I lived upon a cup of slop coffee and the dry, hard crust of bread. This is no exaggeration, as many others can testify to its truthfulness. Coffee was brought over to our quarters in a dirty, greasy bucket, always with grease swimming upon its surface; bread, rotten fish and meat, all mixed together, and thus we were forced to live for months, until starvation nearly stared us in the face.

When the Fifth Artillery arrived and we looked upon the faces of men of our own color and race, we felt greater security for our lives. We did not think it possible that worse men could be found upon the face of the earth than most of the officers connected with the Eighty-second United States Colored Infantry, but we soon found that we had traded off the witch for the devil. As for the enlisted men, or private soldiers, both white and black, I must say that we were treated by them with the utmost kindness and consideration, which shall ever be remembered with the most grateful feelings.

It was but a short period before the hatred of the officers of the Fifth Artillery became visible and felt in more instances than one. Their arrival dated from about November 13, when General Hill assumed command of the post. Frequent visitations were made by them to our quarters without a word being spoken or a question propounded, they looking upon us as if we were wild beasts and concocting some plan to degrade and further torture us.

A Useless Protest.

First Lieutenant William Van Reed, adjutant, being officer of the day, O'Laughlin determined to ask him for the cause of his being placed in irons. O'Laughlin stated to him it was not in conformity with the findings of the court: that sentence did not call for such inhuman treatment at the hands of his jailers, that he had conformed to every requirement since a prisoner in the hands of the government, never violating any rule governing the command and firmly protesting against such barbarous treatment.

Lieutenant Van Reed walked up and down our quarters in his insignia of rank, and replied:

"Sir, your sentence is nothing: we can do with you and to you just as we please," and, without further comment, abruptly left our quarters.

If a subaltern officer could thus set aside the findings of

an entire court of officers, also override the modified sentence of the President of the United States, he possessed more real power over us than either and had it in his assumed power to ignore the findings of the court in its entirety, and, if so desired, could order us on sight to be taken from our cell and executed in like manner to others.

What a parody of justice! Unless that long-drawn-out trial, with its horrors attending for months, its findings to be thus ignored by a subaltern officer in the service of the United States. The time was fast approaching when I, like unto the others, was to be made again to feel the iron heel of the despot sent to overlook and guard us. It could be read in the eyes of each officer as he approached, could be viewed in their many consultations after and during a visit to our quarters, as they slyly gazed from one to the other, after looking upon my unshackled limbs as yet.

Again Put in Irons.

On November 17, 1865, Capt. George W. Crabbe, first lieutenant United States Artillery, came into our quarters accompanied by the sergeant of the guard, and in a very gentlemanly manner thus addressed me:

"Arnold, I have a very painful duty to perform, but I am forced, as you are aware, to carry out and obey the orders from my superiors, no matter how grating against my feelings they may be. I am ordered," he continued, "by Gen. Bennett H. Hill to place you in irons, he having received orders to that effect from higher authority, as turned over to him by Major Wentworth, just relieved in command of the post."

I protested against it as a violation of the organic law of the land, both civil and military, and also of the sentence meted me by the military commission. I informed him that I was a prisoner, it was true, but that no act of my life had justly merited me to be imprisoned, much less incarcerated and weighted down by falling chains, and cried out against such a shameful abuse of power.

He replied that he was grieved to have to perform the duty, but that there was no alternative left but to strictly follow the order assigned him. The sergeant of the guard was then ordered to execute the command, and I was ironed in like manner to the others. We five constituted the chain gang at Dry Tortugas. We were worked by ourselves, denied all intercourse with everyone upon the desolate island, our footsteps always accompanied by an armed guard and forced, in this condition, to perform the most menial and degrading work upon the key.

From November 17 until December 14 my person and the others were dragged here and there, from morn until night, working in degrading chains, made, in every instance that presented itself to perform the filthiest jobs that the provost marshal could hunt up.[2]

Employed as Clerk.

Things continued thus until December 14, when the prisoner employed as clerk to the commanding officer was released from confinement by order from the War Department. I was sent for, desired to furnish a specimen of my handwriting, which I did, and from that date was employed as clerk in the adjutant's office. The noise arising from the clanking chains upon my feet, when walking about the office, soon grated upon the ears of the commanding officer, who, in consequence thereof, in special post order, relieved me from the irons indefinitely, but kept the others still ironed and occupied at labor, as before mentioned.

I had been in the office but a few days when orders were issued which separated me from my only companions upon the island. I was transferred from my dungeon to the general guardhouse, denied communication or intercourse with the few with whom I was individually imprisoned, forced to dwell amid the confusion and noise abounding among numerous sentinels. This was of anything but a pleasant nature to my senses. I could not conceive why I had been relieved of suffering of one kind to have another heaped upon me of just as bad a nature, and I determined, if possible, to have it corrected in some way.

In a communication addressed to the commanding officer I requested to be returned to my former place of confinement, for, although a dungeon, it was far preferable to the guardhouse where I was then confined; that there were no consequences attending the change of situation; that instead of being an amelioration of my condition I found it an aggravation. My request was complied with and I was again placed in the dungeon with my companions, which fact had the tendency to ruffle the disposition of the post adjutant[3] by whose order I had been placed there (without the sanction or knowledge of the commanding officer), as he remarked to me afterwards, stating that he placed me in the guardhouse to prevent the contents of communications received at the office being divulged to the inmates of my quarters.

Together Once More.

From that time out we remained together. The orderly accompanied me to and fro, from my cell to headquarters, and to every point I required to visit. At retreat, or sundown, we were locked together within our dungeon, remaining until carried out to our morning labors at sunrise.

With the arrival of the Fifth Artillery at the post the regulations which had been in force were changed, and cruelty became the order of the day. Not only were prisoners the recipients of it, but to a very great extent it prevailed over the enlisted men, recruits just arrived to fill up the different companies, which had been reduced through expiration of terms of enlistment. There was scarcely a day that passed but that 10 to 15 would be seen, carrying from morning until night heavy cannon balls upon their shoulders, and often continuing for days as well as nights.

To fail to salute an officer was a sure forerunner of punishment, when, in fact, at times it was impossible to distinguish them, they not being clad in their required uniform. The manual of arms was drummed into the recruits with the butt end of the musket, and the different evolutions of the command were first learned in the regions of the back, legs and breast, the drilling officer not being particular as to what part of the body the blow was given. Our close proximity to the guardhouse afforded every opportunity of becoming conversant with the many different acts of cruelty and tyranny practiced, which I will hereafter relate.

Dungeon Was Flooding.

We remained in our dungeon quarters until sometime in the month of February, 1866, at which period our removal took place, arising from the woeful condition of the quarters, it becoming flooded with water to the depth in places of one foot, created by the rains and leakage through the walls. This had been so, more or less, ever since our confinement there, but failed to attract the attention of our jailers until it became so plain that their all-seeing eyes in all else could not fail but to notice it. The health of each had become very much impaired from confinement in this malarious dungeon, and when it was announced that we were to be removed to other quarters we heralded the change with joy, feeling that we would be able to regain our health somewhat by coming in contact with the pure, fresh sea breeze.

In this, however, we were sadly disappointed. Our quarters were placed immediately over the sally-port of the fort, the casements so constructed that we obtained less fresh air and ventilation than in the quarters we had been removed from, and to make it more confined and unwholesome an eight-inch wall was erected between the arch division, dividing the casemates, thereby darkening the quarters and breaking off every particle of air from the sea.[4]

On the water side, fronting our quarters, occasionally a glimpse of the sky above could be had, but beyond this -- nothing. There were three windows, measuring five feet long and six inches in width, set about two or three feet in the wall, distant from the ground floor about seven feet, completely breaking off all view to the outer world and preventing the breeze, so necessary to health, from being obtained. The wall here, as heretofore, was a mass of slime, produced from the dampness of the casemates.

Water Bailed Out.

Often during our confinement in the place buckets were used to bail out the collected water, it having been found necessary to dig deep holes and gutters to catch the water, thereby preventing our quarters becoming flooded all over. For months --- yes, over a year --- were we quartered in this filthy place, having as companions in our misery every insect known to abound on the island, in the shape of mosquitoes, bedbugs, roaches and scorpions, by which, both night and day, we were tormented. Our limbs drawn in different shapes by rheumatism contracted from the dampness, though a wreck, my iron constitution outlived it all.

Conspirators' cell, showing drainage channel in floor

When asking that an ameliorating change be made, no notice was taken thereof; in fact, it grew worse, if possible. A guard stood at our doorway constantly, preventing the approach of anyone to our quarters, excepting when accompanied by the officer of the day, the commanding officer or surgeon of the post. We were made a show of when any Nabob or officers came upon the island, to whom we were not permitted to speak, standing like so many statues in their presence.

Officers whose minds should have been clear to act with justice were reveling in intoxicating beverages, and frequently to such an extent that they dwelt on earth as in a dream, relentlessly carrying to extremes visionary orders under an assumed authority when laboring under impaired functions produced through too copious draughts upon the bottle. The prisoners and soldiers received the full benefit of their wandering minds. The emaciated prisoner could be seen performing his daily labor weighted down in chains, with heavy balls attached. Another, for some supposed dereliction of duty, could be seen marching around a ring under the torrid heat of the sun, weighted down by monster cannon balls upon his shoulders.

Fell Within Their Tracks.

I have seen them fall within their tracks, unable to perform the inhuman duty exacted, from sheer exhaustion, to be then thrust within a dungeon, to remain until strength was sufficiently restored to resume the barbarous task. I have seen them suspended between heaven and earth by their thumbs, and every species of inhumanity that the mind of man could invent was heaped upon both prisoners and soldiers, slaves beneath the petty tyrants' control. This and much more, which I will in due time disclose, was practiced within that stronghold, built to protect freemen and uphold liberty, whilst our starry banner waved majestically in the breeze, emblem of liberty to the world as seen from afar, but beneath which tyranny prevailed, devising means to surpass the cruelties inflicted in barbarous ages.

Our condition remained unchanged until sometime in the month of February, 1866, when a communication was received from the War Department asking to be informed whether or not Dr. Mudd, as reported by his wife, was working in irons, and, if so, to relieve them at once.[5] Orders were received that night to discontinue the irons, and from that period out we were all released from that uncalled for and unsanctioned cruelty and indignity. This, with other communications heretofore mentioned, conclusively established the fact that a base subterfuge had been practiced upon us to gratify alone the evil passions of those who were prejudiced against us.

Shortly after our change of quarters Col. George St. Leger Grenfell, who had been made to bear in part the same harsh injustice as ourselves, wrote a communication to the commanding officer, Gen. B.H. Hill, asking the reason why he had been placed in irons, etc., as the same reasons could not be attributed to him as to the others, from the fact that he was upon Governor's Island[6] at the time Mudd made his attempt at escape, and certainly could not have been connected therewith, nor have any knowledge thereof. In fact, he did not know that there was such a person in existence as Dr. Mudd, and, if there were no just grounds for the irons, he asked that they be struck off and other quarters assigned him.

Relief for Grenfell.

The next day he was relieved of the irons and assigned other quarters, the General having found that there were no orders in his case, after the old Colonel had suffered through their injustice for six months.

The only view from our quarters was the inside of the fort. There were but few things that transpired within its environs but that came under our observation, because directly beneath was the guardhouse, the chief point where the barbarities were practiced and inflicted upon prisoners and soldiers. At this time it was an everyday occurrence to behold men plodding around a ring, both day and night, carrying logs and cannon balls, the balls varying in weight from 24 pounds up to 128 pounds.

To be reported was enough to award punishment, neither soldier nor prisoner being allowed to utter a word in his own defense. To look sideways at an officer was the forerunner of a ball to be carried two hours on and two hours off, frequently for a week or ten days. There was a soldier by the name of Wheeler, Company M, Fifth Artillery, who was required to carry a ball for a month, both day and night, two hours on and two hours off, because he altered his pantaloons furnished by the government, instead of going there to the tailor to have it done, he preferring to do it himself and save the cost of the same, he being a poor man and having a family dependent upon him.

Chapter Eleven

—

CRUEL AND INHUMAN PUNISHMENT

—

Prisoners and Soldiers Alike Are Victims

———

Anything But a Paradise---Grenfell's Joke Not Appreciated---Recruits Were Maltreated---Alleged Inhumanity to a Soldier---A Severe Arraignment---Pvt. Dunn Tied Up to Bell Post---Commander Interfered with Punishment---A Short Respite for Dunn---Prisoner Could Not Hold the Ball---His Cries Were Smothered.

[Monday, December 15, 1902]

During the first year and a half, the Dry Tortugas was anything but a paradise. There did not pass a day but men could be seen tied up by their thumbs, between the sky and the earth, until the joints of their thumbs were nearly pulled from their sockets; some carried to the Gulf Stream, bound in cords and nearly drowned, and others tied up in the guardhouse and lashed upon their naked backs.

Many of these cruelties were inflicted because the victims had followed the example set by some of the officers in charge of them and had dared to become intoxicated. There was another mode of punishment applied in many instances. Men were what they termed nailed to the cross or spread eagle fashion, and others were tied with their hands behind them to swinging limbs, the tip of their toes barely touching the earth. If these same cruelties were practiced in other portions of the Army to the same extent as was done at Dry Tortugas the cause of so many desertions from the service could easily be discerned. Had the soldiers at that post the facilities of deserting there would have been but few of the command left to do garrison duty.

Many left in small boats, to make their way from these scenes of torture, across 200 miles of sea, preferring to risk their lives upon the deep than to remain, daily dunned to death by such brutal measures enforced there. These particular cases I will hereafter refer to, it being my desire, as far as possible, to relate each thing in order, as far as memory can recall.

A short time after Colonel Grenfell's removal to other quarters a case of smallpox broke out upon the island. The patient, instead of being placed in a remote corner of the fort, there being many unoccupied casemates available at the time, where the disease would not endanger others, was brought and placed midway between our quarters and those of Colonel Grenfell. We came in contact with it daily as we passed to and from our labor. Colonel Grenfell receiving the full benefit therefrom upon each puff of wind that passed. We failed to become inoculated with the loathsome disease, however.

Finding the patient still remaining in close proximity to each of our quarters, Colonel Grenfell obtained a large blackboard and upon it in large letters inscribed "Smallpox Hospital," directing all persons on the island to shun it. This drew the attention of the officers, together with the murmurings heard all over the island, and the patient was removed to another portion of the fort. The action of the authorities in this affair was so pointed that not only ourselves, but each man upon the island, firmly believed that it was done for the express purpose of inoculating us with this fearful and loathsome malady.

Joke Not Appreciated.

Colonel Grenfell was severely reprimanded for his action and sternly commanded to take in the board and to be very careful in his actions in the future. He was not in the least intimidated, but strictly garnered the actions of the officers at the fort, recording them in a diary, which he kept during his imprisonment, and which, I learned, is now in the possession of Captain McElrath, Company L, Fifth United States Artillery.[1] At this period sustenance was horrible and of the most disgusting nature. We sustained ourselves from our own resources. It was a godsend that we possessed it, otherwise starvation would have stared us in the face.

Colonel Grenfell's quarters were papered over its woodwork front inwardly with its daily rations of bread and meat, a nail having been placed through it to fasten it to the wall. Soldiers were loudly complaining about their rations and the quality issued. Often when guarding us they requested something to eat, stating that they were nearly starved; that they were robbed of their rations, etc.

Many a one's hunger was relieved by us from our own scant supply, through which we gained their friendliness in some instances, but as a general thing they were kind, and sympathized with us in our misfortunes, and would have permitted us to have escaped if in doing so they would not have been compromised in the matter. They complained bitterly of the distribution of the company fund, stating that the benefit therefrom was not received by them, but used by the company officers themselves. This was the general complaint among them all during the first two years of our incarceration. I make no assertion myself or accusation in this matter, as I am entirely ignorant upon the subject, and I give but the statements of others in this special instance.

Recruits Were Maltreated.

Never were a lot of recruits worse maltreated. They were beaten, bruised and maimed by the harsh treatment and punishment awarded. Inhumanity seemed to be the ruling element, and barbarity and injustice the only thoughts of those in power, our rulers. Sunday morning would always find 20 or 30 packing balls at the guardhouse in the boiling sun until some of them, exhausted and overcome by the heat, would fall in an almost lifeless condition and lie there, no notice being taken of them until after the fact had been reported to the officer of the day, when they would be picked up and conveyed to the hospital for medical treatment.[2]

A French Canadian died about a month after his arrival, superinduced from the cruelties practiced upon him by the first sergeant of his company, receiving knocks on the head, body and limbs from the butt-end of the musket, used until nature gave way, and he was consigned to a premature grave on the adjacent island of East Key. The man who perpetrated this piece of cruelty was afterwards, through examination, made a lieutenant in the United States Army.[3] This was not the only instance of his cruelty, as every soldier who was in the company can testify. He misused, with but few exceptions, every man in the company.

A private soldier of his company by the name of Street[4] came into the hospital one morning while I was there, with the blood streaming down his neck from a wound inflicted at the hands of this sergeant during drill. I saw the man myself and received my information directly from him. I cannot remember the names of the many so ill treated, but they were numerous. In one instance he struck one of the soldiers of his company over the fingers with his sabre, nearly severing them from the hand. Often was I shown, also, by my roommates, deep and black bruises on their bodies.[5]

Alleged Inhumanity.

Another instance of heartless inhumanity was perpetrated upon a soldier in Company D, Fifth Artillery, by name of Christian Conrad, a German.[6] Conrad had been afflicted with fits and suffering so much therefrom that he was unable to perform his duties in his company. He was placed in the hospital. While there his condition grew rapidly worse, the lower portions of his body becoming nearly useless to him, it being with the utmost difficulty that he could drag one foot after the other.

The doctor in charge[7] stated that this was mere pretense, and that he would bring him around to duty. He was discharged from the hospital, placed in the guardhouse and ordered to carry a 24-pound log, which was done under the most excruciating pain, as the man trembled like an aspen all over from the exertion required to execute the imposed task, his limbs being dragged along almost devoid of life or action. During the performance of this task, a cruelty unsurpassed, his frame was violently contorted with repeated fits, the command given being that no soldier should interfere or offer any assistance in the pretended spells, and he was left writhing in his agony without any helping hand being permitted to reach forth to relieve his sufferings.

For a week he remained in the guardhouse, attacked repeatedly with these fits. Buckets of water were ordered to be thrown over him when under their influence, and his condition grew worse and worse. He was again removed to the hospital, where he remained until sometime in November, 1866, when he was discharged from the service of the United States. He was borne upon a stretcher to a steamer lying at the wharf, a helpless man, unable to stand up or move his lower limbs. He frequently expressed the opinion that the doctor was trying to kill him, and whenever the physician made his appearance in his ward his entire frame shook with fright and horror.

Severe Arraignment.

Harshness began to increase in manner, both to the soldiers and prisoners. Drunkenness ran riot on the island. There was not a day passed but that officers could be seen under its influence as they staggered down the walk leading from their barracks to the sally-port of the fort. Gaze where you would, the eye would come in contact with some of them, inebriated, a disgrace and dishonor to the service of the country which they represented.

Liquor was obtained from every boat that entered the harbor, and if the supply became exhausted before the arrival of a boat again inroads were made upon the hospital supplies, so that when needed in case of sickness the supply was exhausted. I state this not upon mere hearsay; I have witnessed all these things myself; have seen orders sent to the hospital for the liquor; have seen the orderly as he returned bearing the bottles; have unwrapped the covering and read the label "Spiritus Fermenti," and have seen the peculiar bottle containing the fluid upon the officers' table.

But with this I have naught to do. If the government permits its officers to live under the influence of liquor and advances supplies for such purposes we, the people, have no right to complain, but must support it. From the barbarous treatment daily received from the officers from under the influence of intoxicating draughts many of the soldiers began to contemplate desertion. Many succeeded in their efforts until it became necessary to restrict them from going to Key West upon passes. Passes of every description consequently were rescinded and soldiers became as much confined on the island as prisoners.

One of the most heartless acts witnessed in this age of civilization happened on the occasion when the paymaster had arrived at the fort to pay off the troops. It was a counterpart of the Middle Ages in cruelty and barbarity. The prisoners were engaged in unloading a vessel moored at the wharf, containing commissary and quartermaster stores for the post. During the work the prisoners, whose duty it was to unload vessels on arrival, indulged freely in spirituous liquors, in company with soldiers who had charge of them. A prisoner by the name of James Dunn became beastly intoxicated in company with two of the soldiers who were acting as provost guards.[8]

Tied Up to Bell Post.

The occurrence was reported to the officer of the day, when he gave the orders to the sergeant of the guard to place him on the ring to carry a ball, but, finding he was too drunk to comply with the order, he ordered him to be tied up. Accordingly, he was tied up to the bell post erected in front of the guardhouse by his wrists, it being about 11 o'clock in the morning.

On returning to my quarters for dinner Dunn was still tied up to the post, remaining there until my return to the office, about 2 o'clock in the afternoon. I returned to my quarters about 5:30 P.M. and found Dunn transferred from the bell-post and tied up by his thumbs to the iron bars or railing immediately beneath our quarters. He was in drunken insensibility, swinging to and fro, bound around by a small rope, his legs stretched outwardly, the whole weight of his body resting upon his thumbs.

The ends of the thumbs were fearfully swollen and puffed out, having the appearance of a mortified piece of flesh. His head was drooping backward, the burning rays of the sun striking him full in the face, and the face red, blue, and in some parts, nearly black, the veins in the neck swollen and extended like cords, there being practically no circulation of blood. I viewed him hanging in this condition until after 5 o'clock.

Commander Interfered.

There is no telling how long he would have remained in this position had not Major General Hill, commanding, happened to pass that way, and, seeing this piece of barbarous cruelty inflicted upon an insensible human being, immediately directed the sergeant to take him down and place him in the guardhouse. He commanded that in the future no man, while in a drunken condition, be punished in like manner. Instead of undoing the cords from his thumbs, they were cut away and Dunn fell heavily upon the ground, not even awakening from the deep stupor as his head came in contact with the hard ground. He was then dragged bodily into the guardhouse, where he remained until retreat.

Gen. Bennett H. Hill

The officer of the day came down to inspect the guard, and, looking around, failed to find Dunn. Inquiring of the sergeant where he was, he was told he was in the guardhouse. The officer ordered that he be taken out and made to carry a ball and lift, the sergeant to execute his order. Dunn was brought out, and, from the tortures already practiced upon him, was unable to clasp the ball, it constantly slipping from his grasp. He essayed to balance it upon his shoulders, to comply with the orders, in his intoxicated condition. In his endeavor to do so he fell twice, once the 42-pound cannon ball falling directly upon his chest, as he fell backwards, and again as he plunged forward, the weight of the ball giving impetus to his fall, he horribly mutilated the entire left side of his face as it plowed through the coral sands.

The sergeant, to execute the orders received, strapped the ball upon his back in a knapsack, but Dunn, staggering here and there, caused the material to give way, which again, when relieved from the weight upon his back, caused him to fall forward upon his face. At this point, the officer arrived, and, seeing the man's lacerated face, ordered him back to the guardhouse, there to remain until 8 o'clock, then to be taken out and made to carry the ball. This scene was witnessed by many persons on the island and the entire crew of the steamer which was lying at the wharf.

A Short Respite.

All of the excitement attending the affair had died away and quiet prevailed throughout the fort, except loud peals of laughter from the officers' quarters, telling in unmistakable terms of the revelry which existed there. The poor tortured drunken victim, with his lacerated hands and face, was temporarily forgotten, but the time was again approaching when they would again place their victim on the rack.

Eight o'clock was pointed by the hands of the clock, and Dunn, to the minute, was led from the guardhouse to renew his task and take his punishment. There were others confined in the guardhouse, all of whom were brought forth and ordered to pick up a ball and carry it. Armed guards were stationed over them to enforce the order, they being authorized to bayonet them in case the orders given were not strictly complied with.

The severity of the punishment already inflicted upon Dunn made it a physical impossibility for him to conform to the orders given. His hands were unable to perform their office. Repeatedly he grasped the ball, only for the hands unconsciously to relax their hold, letting the ball fall to the earth.

When, after repeated efforts, he found it impossible to obey the commands given, the sentinel threatening him with the point of the bayonet if he still persisted in not complying with the orders, in piteous cries he appealed from one to the other, saying to the sergeant, could he, he would willingly carry the ball as ordered.

"Sergeant," he said, "I am willing to carry the ball. God knows the truth of what I say, but I cannot do it. If you do not believe me, come, oh come, look at my bleeding hands."

It was an iron heart to whom he appealed. There was one answer: "You must carry the ball. Sentinel, if he refuses to carry it obey your orders received and run him through with your bayonet."

Could Not Hold Ball.

To prevent this he again tried to carry the ball, but to no avail. The ball fell from his grasp, and as it dropped to the earth he fell with it, crying out: "Sentinel, I cannot carry the ball. Perform your duty -- bayonet and kill me."

The sentinel endeavored in various ways to cause compliance, and failing to move him in the matter, repeatedly pricked him with the bayonet. Finding Dunn did not move from its touch, the sentinel called upon the sergeant of the guard. Cords were again brought into requisition, and in the roughest manner twisted and bound around his bleeding hands, wrists and thumbs. In the midst of his cries of agony, which reached each portion of the fort, his appeals for mercy could be heard. Useless his pleadings, his prayers, his cries, as the form to which he appealed possessed a heart as hard and callous as stone, which had become more hardened through frequent imbibings by him during the day.

There was a gentleman residing with his family upon the island, in charge of the lighthouse, whose family was disturbed by the piercing cries of the tortured man as he screamed out in his agony. He was forced to call upon the officer of the day to ask that other measures be adopted in the manner of punishment. The officer sent forthwith for the sergeant, who received orders and returned to his guard. In a few moments Dunn was removed from the close proximity of Capt. Henry Benner's lighthouse, and retied to a pair of steps by his hands and wrists, his piercing shrieks during the operation filling every space.

Cries Were Smothered.

To smother these cries he was taken down, gagged with

a bayonet and hurriedly hoisted up again. His smothered tones could now alone be heard as he hung suspended between heaven and earth. For the most part of the night he hung in this manner in almost lifeless condition. Next morning at guard mount, while seated on the steps at the guardhouse, I requested that he would allow me to see his hands. I found them swollen and lacerated in many places, having a gangrene appearance, and perfectly helpless, not being able to move them in any particular.

From the guardhouse he was taken to the hospital, placed under medical treatment, where he remained during the period of his confinement, some three or four months. It was decided at one time that it would become necessary to resort to amputation of one of his hands, but, through careful attention paid him, he finally recovered, sustaining the loss of nearly the entire use of his left hand.

Chapter Twelve

COLONEL GRENFELL'S GRAVE OFFENSE

The World Hears His Story

A Communication to a Friend---Trouble Begins Again---The Other Side of the Dunn Affair---A Formal Investigation Takes Place---Arnold Says Denial is "False"---Commander's Orders Were Violated---A Peculiar Happening---A Negro Victim---Colonel Grenfell Ill---He Performed Heavy Labor.

[Tuesday, December 16, 1902]

Col. George St. Leger Grenfell made note of the tortures to Dunn, and in a communication to a friend of his[1] residing in Richmond, Va., gave a truthful and graphic description of the inhuman punishment which was being inflicted upon both soldiers and prisoners. His friend, deeming that the country should be informed, sent the article to a New York newspaper for publication, and in the month of November it appeared in print. By chance one of the officers attached to the garrison had been sent North in charge of four prisoners from South Carolina, and in overlooking the daily paper his eye came in contact with the article.[2]

The officer returned to the fort before the mails had been received at the post, bearing with him the paper containing the article, which he presented to Brigadier General B.H. Hill, commanding. That it was startling news to them proved itself in the rigid search that was made of the effects of the prisoners. Suspicion centered itself upon Colonel Grenfell as its author, and his quarters and his papers were carefully searched, when in a diary kept by him was found a copy of the article sought after.[3]

For the heinous offense of publishing to the world the brutal tyranny existing upon the island he was removed from his quarters and placed within a dungeon in solitary confinement, where he was denied pen, paper or ink, reading matter of every description and all intercourse and communication with everyone at the fort. Small openings which had been left in the construction of the fort for ventilation were tightly boarded up and closed by orders from the commandant. His quarters were visited frequently during the day by the officer of the guard, who caused the person of the colonel to be carefully searched to prevent the secreting of paper, etc.

George St. Leger Grenfell

Truth had awakened them and startled them from their seeming security when finding that the cruelties practiced had been exposed to the country, and they became very careful that it should not again happen. Colonel Grenfell from this time out became the object of all their attention, he being kept closely confined and guarded from the 15th of November, 1866, until September, 1867, in the miserable cell allotted to him, suffering intensely from heart and other ailments arising from his ill-ventilated quarters.

Trouble Begins Again.

Feeling secure, now that the object of their solicitude had been placed beyond the power to do more harm, as they supposed, the cruelties depicted in his published article were again enacted. Private Gosner,[4] of Company D, a mere boy, was cruelly maltreated, his body being covered with bruises received at the hands of a noncommissioned officer of the company. I saw this myself, he having come to my quarters. He disrobed himself to show his bruised person to me.

Duffy,[5] another member of his company, passed through the same ordeal; in fact, these instances were so numerous that it would be impossible to give a full account of them. Suffice it so say they were of daily occurrence, and inflicted by the commands of officers who were more or less under the influence of liquor.

The press of the country soon cried out against these practiced cruelties and demanded that an investigation of the matter should forthwith be made. In the meantime Gen. B.H. Hill, commanding, wrote a denial in toto of the entire article and forwarded the same to the adjutant general, United States Army, assigning many untruths as to the cause which led to its publication by Grenfell.[6] In a very short time after the War Department had been communicated with an officer[7] was sent from General Sheridan's department and ordered to proceed to Fort Jefferson, Fla.

General Hill was absent at the time on leave at Havana, a subaltern officer being in command. The investigation was a farce. Parties desiring to lay complaint were denied speech with the officer, and others were fearful of opening their lips for fear of after consequences. They had become slaves to their tyrant rulers and trembled at their approach. The officers had a picnic over the matter, indulging in frequent draughts from the Old Brown Jug, and in this manner were their cruel acts smoothed over and for the time being hushed up.

Other Side of Affair.

A former company commander, having been placed on detached service, branded the entire article as a lie, as will be seen by the following article published by him in a Philadelphia paper of date July 7, 1867:

"I desire to make a statement through your columns relative to some reports which have been going the rounds of the newspapers in the North. An abstract of a letter purporting to have been written from this post was published in New York, containing false and scandalous accounts of the treatment of prisoners by the officers here. The author of this letter, it is ascertained, is one G. St. Leger Grenfell, an Englishman and an ex-Rebel officer, who is now confined at hard labor for life for infamous crimes. After exhausting every means of procuring his release, this man seems to have hit upon the plan of endeavoring to excite public sympathy in the North and also in England by having published in such papers as were willing to lend themselves to the transaction the statement referred to, in hopes that more active measures would be adopted by his friends in the latter country and elsewhere to effect his release.

"This man has been treated with marked kindness by all

of the officers here, and, by orders of General Hill, a very pleasant and easy duty was assigned him, and greater limits were allowed him than any other prisoner. By some means he secured a medium of corresponding secretly, and an examination of his papers shows that he has forwarded similar falsehoods to various places, and that the letter published in New York was sent through Bradley Johnson, of Richmond, Va.

Formal Investigation.

"An investigation into the subject was made a few days ago by a member of General Sheridan's staff, and full reports have also been forwarded to the War Department to General Hill, which I suppose will be made public in due time, if demanded by the interest of the service. In relation to this subject I will say further that I am in no way concerned in any of the allegations contained in the letter published, and can therefore speak and write freely on the subject.

"In regard to several of the cruelties referred to in that letter and said to have occurred, I have called upon the sergeant and men of my company and questioned the men reported to have been thus maltreated in a public manner, and now unhesitatingly pronounce the whole statement to be false upon the evidence of the parties most vitally concerned.

"Similar investigations have been made by other officers, the result of which tends to show the entire statement, as published, is what is characterized in the communication of this letter -- scandalous and false in the greatest degree."[8]

Arnold Says "False."

Never was a more base falsehood blazoned to the world than that contained in the above communication. His expressions are similar in purport to those written by the commanding officer to the War Department, proving that concert of action had been agreed upon between them. Grenfell, it is true, had not been punished in the inhuman manner cited in his article published; he referred to others than himself, and, as written by him, was correct, far worse than depicted. His efforts in the matter were alone to break up these heartless acts of cruelty and barbarity, which daily were being practiced upon the island, feeling that continuation of them might revert upon his own shoulders, as none knew what a day would bring forth, as every officer seemed to be invested with unlimited authority, practicing every kind of cruelty the mind could conceive of.

It is natural that brother officers would uphold one

another, as the acts of one reflected upon the whole, but doubly the dishonor when he stoops to deception and debasing falsehood. I speak of nothing herein but that can be substantiated by intelligent and respectable witnesses, if living at the present day, and pronounce that Grenfell's statement, with but few exceptions, was truthful in its whole tenor, notwithstanding all that has been said by General Hill and others. Its truth could be seen in all parts of the island.

Punishments heretofore practiced were abolished, ballcarrying and tying men up by the thumbs were strictly prohibited, and for a few months on the island, which had existed as a hell, assumed brighter appearances. The heavy cannon balls were removed from the guardhouse, leaving only a 24-pound shot to be carried by offenders against military rules, and orders were issued from headquarters directing that no man be punished except on orders directly from the commanding officer.

Orders Were Violated.

These orders were daily violated by the company commanders. Private soldiers, instead of being sent to the guardhouse, as formerly, were taken back of the barracks, beyond the observation of the commanding officer, and punished with the usual severity. When it became apparent that the effect of the article published by Grenfell had died out, they gradually increased the punishment, resorting in many instances to the inhuman practice of throwing men into the sea. Drunken men were frequently wheeled to the wharf in a barrow and submerged beneath the water and almost suffocated.

There was a prisoner by the name of Brown who had been suffering from sickness for sometime, and on the morning in question had gone to the doctor's call, and by him had been excused from labor during the day. Contrary to custom, he was ordered out to work by the provost marshal. He stated his case, that he was excused; in fact, that he was so weak that he could not labor, when to cure him of his ailment he was ordered to carry a 42-pound shot. He did as commanded for sometime, until overcome by the sun and his affliction, when he dropped the ball and refused to carry it longer. Forthwith he was bound around the feet, his arms being tied behind him, and he was conducted to the sea and submerged beneath the waves.

The officer in charge[9] repeatedly asked him, when his head was brought above the surface, if he would carry the ball. The man, from swallowing so much salt water, was unable, no matter how much he desired to do so, to give him the required answer, when he was submerged again. Finally, when nearly drowned, he was raised from the water to the wharf, where he remained until sufficiently restored to speak, and, finding it was death by drowning if he refused to obey the order, he acquiesced to the demands, and in his ill condition, his entire clothing saturated with salt water, plodded, more dead than alive, around the ring, with tottering footsteps, carrying the ball until sunset. Then in his wet clothing he was thrust within the guardhouse, to remain during the night, without bed or covering of any kind.

A Peculiar Happening.

Sometime afterwards quite a number of colored prisoners were released by orders from the War Department, many of whom had been waiting upon the officers at headquarters as cooks, waiters, etc. It seemed as if a theft had been committed, in the shape of clothing, money, pistols, etc. by some of them, and before being allowed to leave the island, which was perfectly just, their baggage was searched. Some of the missing articles were found in their possession and they were closely questioned by the officers relative to the other articles, but to no avail.

The Moat at Fort Jefferson

Innocent and guilty alike were marched to the wharf, with General Hill to view with sport, occupying a prominent position on the stern of the schooner *Matchless*, moored at the wharf. Bound up in cords, with their hands, as usual, tied behind them, they were cast into the sea. As they were pushed off the wharf into the sea their cries filled the air, to be suddenly quenched as their bodies sank beneath the waves. This was repeated several times, when they were reconducted into the fort.

General Hill seemed to enjoy the scene wonderfully, his whole frame being convulsed with laughter. After being conducted into the fort a consultation was held among the officers, when one of the prisoners, named James, of Baltimore, from the evidence, being deemed innocent, was released and ordered to do his duties at headquarters. Finally all but one were released, a colored man from Louisiana, who was taken into the guardhouse, his clothing stripped down from his shoulders and back, and given 29 lashes upon the back, laid on well by the enlisted men of the guard.

A Negro Victim.

His cries for mercy as every lash cut into the flesh could be heard in every portion of the fort, gaining force as lash quickly followed lash. After this proceeding, in direct conflict with the laws of the land, the negro remained shut up in the guardhouse, moaning most piteously. The boat being in readiness to leave, he was brought from the guardhouse, marched to the boat and left, with a bleeding and sore back, the shores of the ill-fated island of Dry Tortugas.

The system in our mode of confinement remained unchanged; still guarded and compelled to dwell in our damp and unwholesome quarters when not at work. In the month of January, 1867, a subdistrict having been formed, Brevet Brigadier General B.H. Hill was relieved of command of Fort Jefferson, and assumed command of the subdistrict, with headquarters at Key West, Fla. In the meantime many of the officers composing the command were transferred to other points, and with a light heart every prisoner and soldier watched their departure.

The officers afterwards assigned were of better material and more humane, governing with a rule more adapted to civilization, although, in many instances, acts of barbarity were practiced. After General Hill was relieved of command[10] a gross injustice was enacted on the person of Col. G. St. Leger Grenfell.

Colonel Grenfell for sometime had been complaining very much, this complaint growing out of the harsh and cruel measures resorted to in the manner of his confinement. His dungeon quarters, go past when you would, looked as if water was constantly thrown over the floor -- dampness generated from ill-ventilation. Frequently he could be seen, when permission had been given him, hanging his blankets on the opposite fence to dry, moving along like one writhing in pain, scarcely able to put one foot before the other.

Colonel Grenfell Ill.

This had been the case for a long time; still the Colonel stood up under it. One morning every feature of his face plainly showed his condition, proving in most unmistakable terms that he was quite ill. He had never made it a habit to visit sick-call since incarcerated upon the island, stating as a cause for his not doing so his fear that poison might be administered to him, as every officer was deadly prejudiced against him on account of the articles he had published as to the inhuman tortures inflicted upon soldiers and prisoners.

It seemed that Grenfell had especially created the deep dislike and hatred of each officer from the fact that he had kept from the date of his arrival a diary in which the acts of every officer under his observation had been pictured. This, combined with the other cause before alluded to, made Grenfell's position very insecure.

As before remarked, he visited the sick call, and as his turn came and name called, he presented himself before the Doctor,[11] describing the nature of symptoms of his complaint. Every feature of his face, distinctly showed the truth of his statement. The doctor refused to excuse him from labor, although Grenfell remarked to him that he had eaten nothing for five or six days, and that he was so debilitated and weakened that he could scarcely move. This was the first and last visit made to the sick-call.

Finding that he would be forced to labor in his weak condition in the broiling sun, and knowing his inability to do so, he called upon Lieut. Frederick Robinson,[12] stating his case. He was asked if he had been before the doctor, and replied in the affirmative, but that the doctor had refused to excuse him from labor. Whereupon Lieutenant Robinson informed him that he was powerless to act in the matter; that he could not excuse him without the sanction of the surgeon, as he was placed there to decide whether a man was capable of performing duty or not.

Performed Heavy Labor.

The labor required of Grenfell to perform had been of the heaviest sort, which fact he stated to the provost marshal. As he left the presence of the provost marshal he remarked that he would endeavor to do what he could; that his strength was not sufficient to perform the labor which had heretofore been expected of him, but what he was able to perform he would. The provost marshal placed him at his usual work, but was lenient to him, owing to his advanced age and indisposition, frequently permitting him to sit down to rest himself.

While seated in an exhausted condition upon a pile of lumber he was espied by the provost marshal, who hurriedly walked upon him and desired to know why it was that he was not at work. Grenfell replied that he was unable to perform such heavy work; that it was impossible for him to bend his back, he suffering at the time severely with lumbago, as well as other troubles, but that he would perform any labor assigned consistent with his strength.

The work assigned in this instance was the moving of heavy lumber from one pile and heaping it upon another, a common thing resorted to keep men employed and which required the utmost exertion and strength of the young, much less an old and infirm man like Grenfell. He was ordered to resume the work. Grenfell replied: "Lieutenant, I cannot. Anything I am able to perform I will do it most willingly."

This was all that was needed to fire the blood of his jailer, and, with passion depicted upon his face and fire flashing from his eye, he commanded Grenfell to be taken to the guardhouse and to be tied up. Bound around about the body, from his feet upward to his neck, in cords, he was tied to the same iron bars by which their tortured prisoner Dunn had suffered martyrdom.

Chapter Thirteen
—

A PIECE OF INHUMAN DUTY
—

The Violence of Prison Life
—

Grenfell's Torture, Part Two---Many Watched and Murmured---Murder!Murder!---Arnold's Account Not Vindictive---An Act of Violence---One Guilty; All Punished; "Life Was Held Cheap"---"Supported by Higher Authority"---John Winters Killed---A Fatal Shooting.

[Wednesday, December 17, 1902]

Colonel Grenfell, in his erect position, unable to move hand, foot, or body, remained like a statue during the morning, the piercing rays of the sun shining down in full force upon his venerable gray hairs, he having no covering upon his head to shield it from the sun. His gray hairs should have protected him from such unjust punishment, without taking into consideration the position he had formerly occupied in society, Grenfell being a man of fine intellect and gentlemanly culture. Such feelings were buried, otherwise they might have interposed checks against gratifying their deep-sealed hatred against him.

They could not forget that his was the voice that broke their slumbering security and forced their cruel routine of punishment to be suspended for a time. No body like unto this upon which to vent their spleen and hatred. The moment long hoped for had arrived when he should be made to feel the power he had raised his voice against. The government would support them in any measure they might adopt, Edwin M. Stanton, secretary of war, was the most inveterate enemy of Colonel Grenfell, which fact he was informed of through Sir Robert Bruce, British minister at Washington, D.C., in several communications received.

Grenfell remained during the morning tied up in this condition. After dinner, or about 2 o'clock in the afternoon, three of the officers of the Fifth Artillery marched down to the guardhouse, ordering the sergeant of the guard to undo Grenfell from the iron railings and conduct him to the wharf.[1] Each of these officers was armed with a revolver, loaded with powder and ball. Following in the rear of Colonel Grenfell, bound still armed guards,[2] he was marched to the wharf, where they awaited the arrival of the officers ordained to perform as debasing and damning an act of inhumanity and barbarity as degraded the record of any civilized nation.

Every prisoner and soldier on the outer portion of the fort was commanded to retire within the inclosure of the fort, strict orders having been given the sentinels posted at the sally-port to allow no one to pass from within the fort. Men could be seen steering their footsteps from every direction in obedience to the command. Why all this commotion? The cause of it was soon learned, and many of the soldiers collected around the sally-port to view the proceedings.

Many Murmured.

Murmurs arose on all sides and there was not a voice scarcely but that condemned the whole proceeding. Everything being completed, action soon followed. Colonel Grenfell wished to be informed whether or not it was their wish for him to be submerged beneath the water of the sea. They answered yes, and he plunged from the deck of the scow lying alongside the wharf, and was soon buffeting against the waves.

The provost sergeant, holding on to the end of the rope, repeatedly endeavored to pull him beneath the water with jerks of the rope, but failed, the old man keeping his head above the water. The officers, maddened at their failure, resorted to sure measures to carry out their cruel and inhuman design. A half-breed was sent to the blacksmith shop to obtain heavy pieces of iron, to be used as sinkers on his feet. The sergeant was busily engaged in collecting bricks lying around the wharf.

Grenfell stood undismayed in their midst, looking callously on at the preparations being made to sink him, and, turning to one of the officers directing the proceedings, said:

"Gentlemen, if it is your intention to murder me, do it in a respectable manner, and I will thank you for the act."

One of the officers remarked: "Damn you, you deserve to die for the crimes you have been guilty of."

Grenfell's reply was: "I leave God to judge between us which is the worse, you gentlemen or I."

The colloquy was here cut short, the irons and bricks having been obtained. Weighing upward of 40 pounds, they were tied to the feet of Grenfell. He was then cast into the sea, sinking far beneath its treacherous waves. Just as he was thrown into the sea a small boat, containing some ladies who were on a visit to the fort, was nearing the wharf.

Murder! Murder!!

As their feet touched upon the landing Grenfell's head was raised from beneath the water for him to catch a moment's breath. As they raised his head there rang out in clarion notes from Grenfell "Murder! Murder!" His piercing cry alarmed the ladies, and with quickening footsteps they hastened toward the fort, their hands placed over their ears to drown the horrible cries of murder.

Soon were his cries stifled as his head again sank beneath the water, and when raised up again to catch a breath his voice was stifled. They had nearly completed their inhuman deed, there being but little space left between life and death. In an insensible condition he was hauled upon the deck of the scow, unable to speak, respiration scarcely perceptible, the picture of death itself.

Whilst lying in this condition a lieutenant[3] kicked him in the side, and, accompanied by the other officers, left Grenfell in charge of the guard. As they neared the sally-port, conversing the lieutenant remarked that he would either make Grenfell work or he would kill him.

I viewed the whole proceeding from the casemate window adjoining our quarters, in which we were permitted to remain during the hours of the day. This casemate was the one adjoining that directly over the sally-port, from which the whole front of the fort facing seaward was visible, and in a direct line to the wharf, where the transaction described took place. I afterwards conversed with the soldiers who were compelled to perform this piece of inhuman duty, gaining from them sufficient information to corroborate the evidence of my own eyes.

Not Vindictive.

They may attempt to stamp my rendition as false, as has been done in occurrences of similar purport, but, outside of those personally connected in it, the truth of my assertions can be substantiated by respectable and competent witnesses, if at present living. These pages contain nothing but truth throughout. They have not been written through vindictiveness or malice on my part, but only to show the inhumanities practiced upon the island at that time, which were degrading and most dishonorable of men in a civilized country.

In a short time Grenfell, his footsteps tottering, was conducted to his quarters, supported on either side by a sentinel. He was then placed in his cell, undressed by the soldiers, where he remained during the day, sick almost unto death from the large quantity of salt water swallowed during the drowning process resorted to. From this period he remained in his cell. A few months afterwards all of the officers, with the exception of one,[4] were transferred to other posts, new officers taking their places.

The barbarous acts of cruelty were never to such an extent resorted to thereafter. Major Valentine H. Stone arrived at the post sometime in May, 1867, and assumed command. He was a strict disciplinarian, and caused the officers to stand up to the required regulations guiding the Army. He was not only strict as to the enlisted men, but likewise to the officers, causing each to perform regularly his required duties. He was not only a soldier, but also a gentleman of noble type, honorable and humane. His treatment both of us and Grenfell was very kind. He was the same to each and all who conformed to the rules laid down, punishing no one through hatred or prejudice.

An Act of Violence.

Any violation of the rules was severely punished, no matter by whom, he being no respecter of persons. During the period of his command, which was of short duration, everything progressed most favorably in the garrison, only one case calling for stringent measures to be resorted to. George T. Jackson, assistant military storekeeper, was assaulted by a prisoner named James Orr. Orr was one of the gang of a working party at that time unloading lumber from a schooner lying at the wharf. It was hot, as was the general case on the island, but the men as well as the soldiers had performed the task faithfully.

Jackson happened to run upon Orr whilst seated upon a pile of lumber, resting himself. In a gruff and commanding voice he ordered him to work again, at the same time telling him that he would report him to the provost marshal. To say that he would report him was equivalent to saying that he must carry a ball throughout the night, after working hard during the day, which fact was known to Orr from past experience, and, as it was his fate to be punished, he determined to work very easy at his assigned task.

As ordered, he proceeded to his work as usual, no doubt studying out some mode of procedure to avenge himself upon Jackson. As Jackson was called away sometime afterwards to execute some order, Orr had matured his plan. On his return towards the boat Jackson was met by Orr, who stated that there was an officer desirous of seeing him back of the stable. Jackson started to see the person, Orr following close behind him. He turned upon Jackson finally, inflicting a severe wound upon his face with a penknife in his hand.

One Guilty; All Punished.

Jackson fled toward headquarters, the blood gushing from the wound inflicted at the hands of Orr, and reported the occurrence to the commanding officer. The affair created intense commotion, and Orr was immediately arrested by the guard and confined. No doubt Orr fully intended to kill him, as he struck the blow, and deserved due punishment for the crime. Yet I could not feel that for his offense every other man confined should have been made to suffer. About a month after the occurrence, Major George P. Andrews arrived and assumed command of the post. The facts in the Orr case were communicated to him, whereupon he issued the following post order, making every man's life insecure; in fact, empowering any ill-minded sentinel to take one's life. I furnish herewith an extract or copy of the order as promulgated, and through which one man lost his life:

Headquarters, Fort Jefferson, Fla.
June 11, 1867

Special Order No. 78

EXTRACT.

3. The attention of the officers of the post is called to the fact that atrocious crimes have been committed by prisoners at this post, who seem to think that they cannot be reached by the law. In future every sentinel must use his bayonet and cartridge, and no sentinel who faithfully tries to do his duty shall ever see the inside of the guardhouse. If a prisoner refuses to obey orders the sentinel must shoot him and then use his bayonet, at the same time calling for the guard. The responsibility for obedience to this order will be borne by the commanding officer.

By order Major George P. Andrews, Comd'g Post.

(Signed)   PAUL ROEMER
First Lt. 5th Arty., Post Adjutant

"Life Was Held Cheap."

After the issuing of Special Order No. 78 a man had to be

very particular and careful, as his tenure of life hung upon slender threads. The sentinel held within his hands the life of every individual over whom he stood guard. To gratify his own feeling of hatred or revenge he was invested with the power to kill his victim, under cover of faithful execution of his duty, assigning cause for his deed a refusal on the part of the victim to comply with orders given. Neither in a civilized nor uncivilized country did there emanate such an atrocious order, sanctioning murder.

It was a stigma and a disgrace upon the nation which they represented. I do not attach any blame to Major Andrews in the matter, for, from what I heard him remark on one occasion, of which I will speak hereafter, he received his orders from a higher source, from Edwin M. Stanton, secretary of war. Punishment of severity soon became the order of the day. Trivial offenses were soon punished by the carrying of a 128-pound cannon ball from one place to another and back again, through which many men became injured.

I will not state the remark Major Andrews made, which gives the authority for the issuance of the infamous order heretofore alluded to. I was on my way to headquarters one afternoon, and as I turned to go up the path leading to the barracks I came in contact with a soldier named Fisher,[5] of Company I, who was straining and tugging to raise a 128-pound ball upon his shoulder, a sentinel with loaded musket standing over him. As I neared him Major Andrews turned from the garden and, approaching Fisher, who as yet had been unsuccessful in raising the ponderous shot upon his shoulder, commanded that he should carry the shot, instructing the sentinel at the same time to shoot and bayonet him if Fisher failed to comply with the order.

"Higher Authority."

He informed the sentinel that he would protect him in the premises, for, said he, "I am supported by a higher authority, Edwin M. Stanton, secretary of war."

Fisher replied to the commanding officer that it was very hard to be shot down and bayoneted for not obeying that which it was an impossibility for him to perform, but that if he would grant him the right to wheel them into a barrow he thought he might raise them to its bed and execute his behests, stating at the same time: "I do not refuse, Major, to comply with your orders. Sir, it is because nature has not endowed me with sufficient strength to raise a 128-pound ball upon my shoulder."

Fisher was of a very frail and delicate form, and had lost

what little strength he once possessed through the miserable subsistence issued, and the climate itself having to a great degree a tendency to debilitate the strongest constitutions. His request was granted, and thus was saved from death this poor individual, for had he refused to obey the order the sentinel would have carried out his instructions to have saved himself from dire punishment. The punishment inflicted at this period consisted alone in the carrying of those immense balls.

Men could be seen daily straining every muscle and nerve in their forms executing this fearful task, the number required to be carried varying from 25 balls up to the number of 100 for the slightest dereliction of duty. This continued up to the latter part of July, 1867, when a terrible punishment was inflicted upon a drunken prisoner, resulting in his death in the brief space of half an hour. He was the first and the last victim under the infamous Special Order No. 78.

John Winters Killed.

John Winters, a prisoner confined for desertion, was shot down on July 31, 1867, within the inside limits of the fort, whilst in a state of intoxication bordering on insanity, by a private soldier[6] stationed at Post 5, at the bastion leading to the casemates, where the prisoners were confined. This soldier was at one time confined in the guardhouse, charged with sleeping on his post, also with theft.

Whilst confined under these charges the same man whom he shot (Winters) bought from his own limited purse articles of food, cooking it, and furnished him with it. Winters was a harmless man, one possessing a very kind heart, and generous to a fault, but, like some men under the influence of liquor, was boisterous and unruly, but not quarrelsome. He had managed on this occasion to obtain liquor through his intimacy with the soldiers of the garrison.

In going to his quarters, at retreat, he gave two or three drinks from the bottle in his possession to the soldier, standing on his post, and thence going to his casemate. When the private was placed on guard again he called to Winters, asking him to give him another pull, as it was termed among them. Winters told him that he had no more -- that it was all gone.

The soldier hooted at the idea, remarking: "All right, I'll remember you for it." About 11 o'clock Winters became noisy in his quarters and the sergeant of the guard and a file of men arrested him and marched him to the guardhouse. Winters used abusive language to the sergeant, which aroused his passion to a great extent, but at this time took but little notice of the occurrence. About 15 minutes after being confined Winters requested to be allowed to go to the bastion, which was granted, the sergeant ordering the soldier not to permit him to go into his room.

A Fatal Shooting.

Winters eluded the vigilance of the sentinel and returned to his quarters, when a sergeant,[7] in charge of the guard, with a file of men, rearrested him. In passing the soldier the sergeant gave him instructions that if Winters attempted to run by his guard to shoot him. Winters was entrusted to a file of men, some going before and some after him. He was placed ahead of the guard, and, in descending the bastion, unconscious of his impending doom, in his drunken condition he ran out of the doorway into the limits of the fort, when the soldier, who had left his post by many yards, raised his gun as Winters passed him and shot him down, from the effects of which he died in the course of 30 minutes.

The soldier never challenged, neither did he cry "Halt," but deliberately carried out the orders received from the sergeant. The whole garrison was aroused by the report of the gun, coupled with the agonizing cries from the wounded man, who, in his dying moments, requested them to kill him to relieve him of his sufferings. A consultation was then held by the sergeant and the soldier, he having been relieved from his post to arrange the tale that was to be told relative to the shooting. I could not hear much of what had passed, but I distinctly heard of a man[8] who in a very short time thereafter was made corporal state that each must tell the same tale.

While the sergeant had gone for the officer of the day, Winters' piteous moans, mixed with shrieks and heartrending cries, resounded throughout the fort. Life was fast ebbing out, and by the time the officer of the day[9] arrived nothing could be heard but his smothered groans. A stretcher was procured and the dying man conveyed to the hospital, and in a brief space of 30 minutes his spirit had passed from earth to eternity.

When the news of the affair reached headquarters, the loud, ringing voice of an officer was heard crying out, "That's the way we do things in California."[10]

Chapter Fourteen

—

DEATH IN THE TROPICS

—

Yellow Fever Brings A New Terror to Fort Jefferson

—

Dr. Smith First to Succumb---Had Coffins Ready---Fear Reigned Supreme---Cellmates Treated Dr. Mudd---A Talk With Notary---A Threat to Shoot---Old Commander Returns---Grenfell's Bold Escape.

[Thursday, December 18, 1902]

In the brief space of a month after the killing of Winters our small island and inclosure was visited by yellow fever. It made fearful ravages among the limited number stationed there, sweeping nearly every officer at the post away. It struck from earth our best officers and permitted the heartless ones to recover, to repeat again, I suppose, more of their cruelties upon humanity under their command. The ways of Providence are mysterious, and no doubt it was done for some good and wise purpose.[1]

Among the first to succumb to the dread disease was Brevet Major J. Sim Smith, surgeon in charge. Dr. Smith, on his arrival at the post, which was but a few months before, corrected in various instances the abuse and reigning terrors which abounded there. He was, indeed, a man of humanity and kindness, a gentleman by birth and culture -- the soldiers' and prisoners' friend and protector, and, his memory lives in the mind and the heart of all by whom he was then surrounded as all that was good, pure, upright, and noble. He worked with untiring zeal whilst the fever raged, until the fatal malady struck him down upon the bed of sickness, where he lingered but three days and died. He received every attention from Dr. Mudd, who, at that period, had charge.[2]

Mrs. Smith was lying in an adjacent room, sick with the fever. Dr. Mudd paid her every attention and worked unfalteringly to save her life. His efforts were crowned with success and she recovered from the disease. During the period of the sickness of Dr. Smith and family there was neither an officer nor an officer's wife that came near them to administer to their wants, their cases devolving upon the care of Dr. Mudd, and faithfully did he perform all that lay within his power.

In a short time the fever proved epidemic, and men could be seen falling down in every section of the fort, as the dread malady seized them. When in former times officers were parading about devising plans wherewith to torture the soldiers and prisoners nothing was seen or heard of them, they keeping themselves closely closeted, a pall like unto death seemingly hanging over the officers' quarters. Fear was depicted upon the countenance of everyone on the island, each looking for his turn next.[3]

Two of the companies were removed to the adjacent islands, thereby being saved from the fever's fearful ravages. Two companies were retained to guard the fort and prisoners. Prisoners had to stand the brunt of the fever, their only safety being in an overruling Providence. Out of the 52 prisoners confined there but two died, whereas the garrison lost in officers and men 37.[4]

Had Coffins Ready.

Men at first, when taken sick, were carried to the small key termed Sand Key, upon which a small temporary shed had been erected as a hospital, the commanding officer thinking thereby to prevent the garrison from being infected. Sick patients, seated in a small boat, were conveyed over, confronted by coffins which were piled up in the bow of the boat. This of itself was sufficient to cause alarm, and even to kill the faint-hearted, of whom there were quite a number collected on that small area of seven and a half acres.

With but a few exceptions those who were conveyed to the key in the small boat fell victims to the disease, and are buried beneath the sandy soil. When Dr. Mudd was given charge he stated to the commanding officer that it would be advisable to discontinue this practice; that the fever was in our midst, and that it could not be dislodged until the poison had expended itself, advising that all cases be brought to and treated at the hospital. This was acceded to, and, from his manner of treatment in the disease, a great change was soon to be noted.

From this period until the arrival from Key West of Dr. Whitehurst[5] everything was progressing favorably, no death occurring. Dr. Whitehurst, perfectly conversant with the mode of treatment, he having had immense practice in the disease, approved Dr. Mudd's manner of treatment, and it was continued throughout the period the fever raged in our midst. The fever began to assume a more virulent type, and in spite of the untiring exertion of both began to make sad inroads into our numbers.

Everyone now thought of self alone. There was not respect shown by the attendants, they being soldiers taken from different companies, to either the dead or the dying. No sooner had the breath left the body than it was coffined and hurried over to its last resting place, there being a boat, with a crew, detailed as the burying party, always awaiting. In many instances coffins were brought into the hospital and placed alongside of the bed to receive the body of some one expected to die, and had to be removed again, the patient still tenaciously clinging to life.

Fear Reigned Supreme.

Men less sick were startled viewing these proceedings, it having a tendency to cause their own condition to become worse. During the terrible ordeal of the fever the garrison kept itself, duties being neglected by both officers and soldiers. During its progress the island assumed a different aspect. The island, which before was more like a place peopled by fiends than anything else it could be compared with suddenly became calm, quiet and peaceful. Fear stood out upon the face of every human being.

Some attempted to assume the tone of gaiety and indifference, but upon their faces could be read traces of other feelings. For two months the fever raged in our midst, creating havoc among those dwelling there. During this time Dr. Mudd was never idle. He worked both day and night, and was always at post, faithful to his calling, relieving his sufferings of humanity as far as laid within his power. The fever having abated through the want of more subjects, a contract physician from New York arrived at the post and relieved Dr. Whitehurst of his duties.[6] When the new doctor took charge there were but two or three sick, and they were in a state of convalescence.

Soon thereafter Dr. Mudd was taken down with the fever in his quarters, and during the entire period of his illness was never visited by the New York doctor, the surgeon in charge, he remaining closeted in his room. The only medical treatment received by Dr. Mudd during his illness was administered at the hands of Spangler and myself.[7] True, neither of us knew much about the disease or its treatment, all the experience either possessed being derived from observation during its prevalence, and the mode of treatment having been learned from personal experience in the nursing of patients under our charge.

Treated Dr. Mudd.

Dr. Mudd was watched over by us both day and night in turns. We adopted the same method of treatment in his case as had been administered by him in ours, through which he happily recovered. He stated upon his recovery that had it not been for our care and watchfulness he would have died, and thanked each of us in unmeasured terms for our friendly consideration.

Dr. Mudd had worked during the prevalence of the yellow fever with an unfaltering zeal, until nature was well-nigh exhausted, relieving in every way at his command and knowledge the sufferings of humanity, but when afflicted himself he was left entirely to the mercies of his God and the limited knowledge of his two companions, which fact had the appearance of a desire for his death on the part of those at the head of affairs.

Michael O'Laughlen, victim of Yellow Fever

We felt from the first that we had been transported to Dry Tortugas to fall victims to the many dreadful poisons of malaria generated in that climate. Happily we lived through it all, and I am permitted to give to the world at large some inkling of the many wrongs, tortures and sufferings inflicted upon us during the period of nearly four long years of exile. In the month of October, 1867, the fever having exhausted itself and finally stamped out, and with it, to a great extent, the harsh and rigorous measures which had heretofore been adopted in the manner of our imprisonment, some of the privileges which we had taken during its prevalence were curtailed, but for the most part the others were not countermanded by the officer in command.

The officers who garrisoned the fort at this time, with the exception of two, fell victims to the disease. A lieutenant[8] recovered alone through the kind care and watchful nursing and attention of Colonel Grenfell, who remained with him day and night, administering to his slightest want.[9] The officers who died of the disease were coffined and borne to their last resting place by the prisoners of the post, no respect being shown by the other officers. Even wives were carried in like manner to the grave, the husband remaining in his quarters.

Everything went on smoothly after the fever until the month of December, 1867, when there arrived upon the island a notary public, purporting to be from the State of Florida.[10] His business at first was unknown, as it frequently happened that strangers came into our midst on a visit to the commanding officer. His business, however, was soon made known to us. We were ordered separately into his presence, and found he was one of the commissioners appointed by the congressional committee to investigate into the particulars connected with the assassination of President Lincoln.

Letters were shown us as coming from Benjamin F. Butler authorizing the notary to obtain our voluntary statements, etc. We were forced into his presence --- did not go voluntarily --- accompanied by an armed guard. When I was sent for by him and seated he handed me his credentials to peruse, which I carefully did. I returned them to him, stating that I knew nothing concerning the business he was upon; that a statement of all the facts that I knew of had been placed in the hands of the government upon my arrest, and that the government was perfectly conversant with all the knowledge that I possessed, and, from my trial, knew more than I or anyone else did supposed to be connected therewith, and refused to make any further statement.

A Talk With Notary.

I informed him that he was a stranger to me; that he might be as base as those who had already dealt with me; that I did not trust him nor any other man, etc., stating that a burnt child dreaded the fire. He told me to consider it, and I was dismissed and sent to my quarters. After conversing with my roommates over the matter we each arrived at the conclusion that it could do no harm to us, nor the living nor the dead, and concluded to conform to his request.

I called, however, upon the commanding officer, Major

George P. Andrews, and stated my situation to him. I told him that I was a prisoner under his charge, and, as such, demanded his protection. He told me that I should have it, and, thus feeling safe, I gave a statement of similar purport as that first made.

During its writing the notary held out every inducement to cause not only myself, but the others, to swear falsely, stating that if we could implicate any others we would be released from our imprisonment and carried to Washington as witnesses. His advent was about the time of the attempted impeachment of Andrew Johnson, president of the United States, and his visit alone was to attempt to cause us to falsely implicate Andrew Johnson in the assassination.

There was a great deal of unpleasantness pervading our interviews, and high words followed when he wished me to append my signature to an affidavit drawn up by himself. Throughout my statement he attempted to place his construction upon it, and obliterated my writings, until finally I requested to be informed whether he came to write my statement himself or did he come to obtain mine. I refused to sign my name to his affidavit, as drawn up by himself, stating that it inferred that of which I knew nothing. He handed it to Major Andrews, who was seated in the room, to read. The Major could not see it in the same light that I did, stating that it was all correct, etc.

Seeing that neither justice nor protection would be given me, I stated that I would not sign it, and if he was not satisfied I would destroy that which I had written and end the interview; that I asked alone for my rights and protection in them from the commanding officer.

A Threat to Shoot.

Major Andrews immediately rose up and spoke thus:

"Sir, I will take you out on the parade grounds and shoot you."

I replied: "I am your prisoner, Major; you certainly can do with me as you please, and if you deem you have the authority to shoot me, all that is left, me, sir, I suppose, is to stand it."

I was not shot, however, neither did I sign my name to the affidavit, but wrote out one that suited my way of thinking, also wrote my own statement without the notary's assistance, and in the end complied with his request, giving my statement.

I was quite ill before I had completed it, and was annoyed by this man until he nearly worried me to death, the surgeon repeatedly cautioning him not to visit me in my low condition.

He came in spite of all these things, Colonel Grenfell writing my expressions down for me, my condition being such that I was unable to raise my head from my pillow. The same was likewise done to the others, and he left the post much disappointed, as I afterwards learned from some of my friends in Key West.[11]

After he had left the post we were informed through reliable authority that he was armed with the power in case we refused to furnish him our statements to place us in solitary confinement and to be fed upon bread and water, whereas by his papers exhibited to us he was to obtain our voluntary statements. There was nothing voluntary upon our part throughout the whole affair, but force in every instance was used and threats made, besides the inducements held out to swear falsely in the premises.

Old Commander Returns.

Our condition from this time on remained unchanged until March, 1868, when Major Andrews was relieved of command of the post. Col. George St. Leger Grenfell's inveterate enemy[12] was ordered back to the fort and assumed command. At the same time a new provost marshal was appointed.[13] Between the pair the island became a hell again, they devising measures to make prisoners uncomfortable and imprisonment more galling.

As soon as the new commander assumed the reins of power the tendency to persecute Grenfell became apparent, it having been stated to me by Major Andrews, before departure, that his successor felt very bitter toward Grenfell on account of the article published by him, it nearly being the means of his dismissal from the service.

When the provost marshal found prisoners contented and obedient some new order was issued to awaken them from it. He picked as provost guards the most contemptible men of the garrison, who abused, cursed, struck and maltreated the prisoners under their charge in every conceivable manner. Colonel Grenfell, finding, as he afterwards expressed to me, that they had started upon him to kill him inch by inch, determined to attempt escape at all hazards, preferring, as he said, a watery grave to the indignities imposed upon him.

Grenfell at this time had charge of the small garden lately made within the inclosure of the fort. The major, on assuming command, relieved Grenfell from this duty, and placed the old man at the heaviest work that was to be done. Each day was productive of changes and each change bred a worse condition.

Finding persecution setting gradually in upon him more

and more, Grenfell went cautiously to work with others and soon succeeded in making arrangements to escape. There was a soldier by the name of William Norrell who had received very harsh treatment and was anxious to desert. With this man Grenfell formed his plans, in combination with another soldier of the same company.

Made Bold Escape.

On the night of March 6, 1868, their plans were completed. Norrell was a sentinel on Post No. 2, guarding the small boats within the boom. At 10 o'clock at night he went on duty, and Grenfell, with three other prisoners, succeeded in eluding the sentinel within the fort, making their way to the northwesterly side, letting themselves down through one of the portholes into the moat, thence to the breakwater wall, where they walked to the appointed rendezvous, arranging all the necessary articles of food and water for their perilous undertaking.

The night was pitch dark and a furious gale raged at the time, which had existed for six consecutive days. Never did men venture on a more perilous undertaking. The white-capped waves rose even within our sheltered harbor to fearful heights, but beyond in the Gulf, during the day, they reached to mountain heights.

The sentinel waited until 11 o'clock was called, and then embarked with Grenfell and the others in a small boat picked out for the purpose, and soon, with sail set, fled from their ocean-bound home. No one as yet outside of my roommates and myself knew anything of it. The hour of 12 arrived, when the sentinel on Post No. 1 cried out the hour. No sound came from Post No. 2. No. 1 again cried out the hour, and yet no sound from Post No. 2.

The corporal, with a witness, advanced stealthily upon the post, expecting, no doubt, to find the sentinel asleep, a subject for court martial. Behold his amazement when no sentinel could be found. He forthwith returned to the guardhouse, reported the fact to the sergeant, who in turn reported to the officer of the day. Soon there was a commotion all through the fort, men hurrying here and there in search of the missing man, and then to the prisoners' quarters in search, being assured that an escape had taken place.

After diligent search it was found that Grenfell and others were missing, and, on looking into the boom, they realized the means in accomplishing it. Norrell deserted his post, carrying his gun and equipment with him.

Everything remained quiet during the remainder of the

night, but the next morning the fort within was all bustle and preparation for pursuit. There was a steamer lying in the harbor at the time, the commander of which readily consented to go on the search, and about 8 o'clock she steamed out after the escaped party. After cruising nearly the entire day they failed to hear or see anything of the escaped party, and the steamer returned into the harbor again.

Chapter Fifteen

—

FREEDOM, AT LAST

—

A Pardon from the President

—

*Bearing the Brunt of Grenfell's Escape---Alabama Men Aided by Friends---
Arnold Asked for Accusers---Obstruction in Casemate Removed---The Official
Pardon---Room for Uncertainty of Guilt---Truth, Not Malice---Will History
Lie?*

[Friday, December 19, 1902]

When the commanding officer found that Grenfell and
the other escaped prisoners had not been overhauled he issued
the most stringent orders against the remaining prisoners. No
one after retreat was permitted to place his head out of the
aperture of his casemate, under the penalty of having a musket
ball sent crashing through the brain. All intercourse between
soldiers and prisoners was strictly prohibited, a violation of such
order being at first severely punished, and repetition leaving
them open to be arraigned before a court-martial. Many orders
were issued without sense or reason in them.

The escape of Grenfell was another blow struck the
commander, who felt dubious about his commission. Consequently, something had to be done to exonerate himself from all
blame. He communicated to headquarters that Grenfell had
been furnished with means by outsiders, which had been used
in bribing the sentinel; also that he had considerable money in
his possession when he escaped.[1] This was not so. Grenfell did
not have in his possession at the time of his escape $25. He
could have gone without a dollar, as the rule of the place was as
disgusting to the soldier as it was to those confined, and help at
any time would have been rendered to any man who desired to
escape, providing that the soldiers in so doing were not compromised.

The remaining prisoners had to bear the brunt for the
escape of Grenfell and the others. They were worked from
sunrise to sunset in the heat of the broiling sun, a provost

guard, with the commanding officer and the provost marshal, more frequently than otherwise, standing over them and hurrying them up. Not a moment's rest was allowed during the day, excepting at dinner hour, and this continued until the Fifth Artillery was relieved, on March 10, 1869.

Seven prisoners were sent there from Eutaw, Ala., for the alleged offense of threatening to ride a carpet-bagger on a rail. On them was centered a deep hatred and prejudice. They were termed Ku-Klux by the provost marshal for the purpose of engendering hatred in the hearts of the soldiers against them, in which it failed to some extent. Their stay was short, owing to the press of the country taking the matter up, but their manner of treatment was cruel, unjust and tyrannical in the extreme.

When they were torn from their homes and families supplies of every kind were denied them. They suffered from indignities heaped upon them all along the route from Eutaw to Dry Tortugas, weighted down in chains and most spitefully used by those in charge of them. As a matter of course, they were without money, and when released they asked for transportation and subsistence to their homes, which was denied them. They were taken to Key West, an island in the sea, and there, among strangers, were left to make the best of the situation that they could.

Aided by Friends.

From them I learned that they met with friends (all being Freemasons) and, without the assistance of the government, safely arrived at their homes. But a short time after the departure of the prisoners from Eutaw, Ala., it was reported that some parties had been overheard to express an opinion as to how easy a matter it would be to break through their quarters into one of the soldiers' company quarters some night, seize their guns when the whole garrison, excepting those on duty, was at the theater, overcome the guard and seize the quartermaster's schooner *Matchless*, moored at the wharf, raise anchor, cut ropes and put to sea.

This rumor reached the ears of the provost marshal, so said, when in a trice the most stringent measures were adopted to frustrate the design. Double sentinels were placed over the prisoners' quarters, and every privilege formerly granted was rescinded. Myself and companions became the recipients of a necessity created only to persecute. From the first touch of the hand of the military branch of the United States we had received the full weight of their cruelty and tyranny; we had been made to study the effects of partial and then of total darkness, of damp and loathsome cells, of foul and filthy dungeons, of tortures, irons and chains, of degradation of all kinds, and now we were forced to study branches of a more edifying nature, as we were boarded up and denied the pleasure of looking upon mother earth and the few green spots of vegetation growing within the inclosure of the fort, the only visible parts of the creation left us to observe being the overhanging sky and the boundless deep. They determined by such procedure and action that we should have become learned in astronomy and navigation.

This unjust proceeding on the part of those ruling not only deprived our quarters of proper ventilation but caused the dampness to increase, and at the same time had a tendency to cast odium upon us alone. Every person in and out of the fort was confronted with it, and naturally were led to inquire why of all quarters this alone was boarded up.

Asked for Accusers.

As no cause had been assigned for this un-looked for and sudden display of hatred of the provost marshal, we applied to the commanding officer to be informed as to what offense we had committed to justify such action and whether he was acting upon secret information, and, if so, we desired to be confronted with our accusers, knowing that we had neither infringed upon the rules governing nor contemplated any unlawful undertaking.

We were informed that we were not accused of anything, but that the rumor was current of the contemplated escape of some of the prisoners, and that the boards were placed up to prevent prisoners from crossing the guardhouse shed to the corridor beyond, thence into the inclosure of the fort. A poor excuse was better than none. Immediately below our quarters was stationed the whole guard and two sentinels guarded all exits from the fort, who had full view at all times of our immediate quarters, which would have rendered it impossible for anyone to have crossed over. Even had it been possible to have eluded the vigilance of the sentinels at this point, they would have been forced to have come in direct contact with the entire guard as they descended the steps leading to the ground-work of the inclosure of the fort.

Finding that we could not accomplish having the boards removed, we became resigned to the new order of things, never afterward asking any questions relative to it. This continued until a few days before our departure from the island. When it became known that Dr. Mudd had been pardoned and the Fifth

Edman Spangler

Artillery had been relieved Spangler requested that the portion of the fence directly in front of our quarters be removed, so that we could obtain light and proper ventilation to our room, the side walls of which were hung with deep masses of slime and spongy substance, created through extreme dampness.

Obstruction Removed.

The provost marshal said that he would consult General Hill, then commanding, in regard to this request. He did so, and the following day the obstruction was removed. Very soon afterward we received the news of our pardons, when we became callous to all surroundings, feeling that their tenure of persecution and intense hatred which had existed for four years was drawing to a close. Before the departure of the Fifth Artillery we received a telegram notifying us of our pardon, whereupon we received the congratulations of each officer of the post, whether real or fictitious it is beyond my power to state.

On March 29, 1869, having received my release from their custody by virtue of the official pardon granted by Andrew Johnson, president of the United States, issued in our respective cases, we departed from the fort, transportation alone being furnished as far as Key West, Fla. The government had deported us far from our homes to a strange land and had discharged us with no means at command to return. Had it not been for my father, who came for me, I would have been left penniless among strangers, without means to reach my home or to purchase subsistence to alleviate hunger. Like justice followed my footsteps from its beginning to its end.[2]

The Official Pardon.

Armed with the official authority which restored me again to the world a free man, a pardon granted by the United States government, a copy of which is herewith appended, to wit:[3]

Andrew Johnson,
President of the United States of America.
To all to whom these presents shall come, greeting:

Whereas, On the 30th day of June, in the year 1865, one Samuel B. Arnold was, by the judgment of a military commission, convened and holden in the City of Washington, declared guilty of the specification wherein he was charged in the words and figures following, to wit: And in further prosecution of said conspiracy the said Samuel Arnold did, within the military department and the military lines aforesaid, on or before the 6th day of April, A.D. 1865, and on divers other days and times between that day and the 15th day of April, A.D. 1865, combine, conspire with and aid, counsel, abet, comfort and support the said John Wilkes Booth, Lewis Payne, George A. Atzerodt, Michael O'Laughlin and their confederates in said unlawful, murderous and traitorous conspiracy and the execution thereof as aforesaid; and

Whereas, The sentence imposed by said military commission upon the said Samuel Arnold was that he be imprisoned at hard labor for life, and the confinement under such sentence was directed to be had in the military prison at Dry Tortugas, Fla., and the said Samuel Arnold has been for more than three years and six months, and now is, suffering the infliction of such sentence; and

Room for Uncertainty.

Whereas, The evidence adduced against said Arnold before the said military commission leaves room for uncertainty as to the true measure and nature of the complicity of the said Arnold in the said murderous and traitorous conspiracy, and it is apparent that the said Arnold rendered no active assistance whatsoever to the said Booth and his confederates in the actual execution of said abominable crime; and

Whereas, The pardon of the said Arnold is strongly recommended by the City Council and more than two hundred other citizens of Baltimore and vicinity;

Now therefore, be it known that I, Andrew Johnson,

President of the United States of America, in consideration of the premises, divers other and sufficient reasons me thereunto moving, do hereby grant to the said Samuel B. Arnold a full and unconditional pardon.

In testimony whereof I have hereunto signed my name and caused the seal of the United States to be affixed.

Done at the City of Washington this first day of March, A.D., 1869, and in the independence of the United States the Ninety-third.

ANDREW JOHNSON.
President of the United States.

WILLIAM H. SEWARD.
Secretary of State.

I was at last a free man.

Truth, Not Malice.

I have in the foregoing pages strictly confined myself to the truth, compiled from a diary as daily taken note by me. It has not been written through malice nor vindictiveness on my part, but solely for the purpose of giving to the world the manner of treatment adopted and pursued in my respective case, both during the period awaiting trial, throughout the trial itself, and even after the sentence had been imposed. Also relative to the treatment of others undergoing sentence and confined at Dry Tortugas, Florida.

The hatred engendered by the Civil War had not yet abated. The crime in which I was supposed to have been connected, and for which I was imprisoned, was of such an abominable and atrocious nature that the hatred which at first had been instilled into the hearts of the entire nation did not subside during the entire incarceration. They looked upon me as a monster, from the sentence imposed by the Military Commission, and nothing could be brought to bear to change or modify their deep-rooted convictions.

Not even the government nor those in high authority could be appeased, and they still persecuted, even after the sentence had been imposed, and would have continued to do so had I remained under their charge. To have obtained justice at or about the period of my trial was an impossibility, as well as a fruitless undertaking, whilst the public mind was in such chaotic excitement and frenzy. Evidence was hardly necessary to convict. The desire was only to gratify and appease the public mind, and to avenge the death of Abraham Lincoln.

The crime in itself was of such a base, cowardly, damnable and atrocious nature that it necessitated harsh measures, yet justice should have interposed its hand, separating the innocent from the guilty, which was not performed in the beginning, nor through the entire period of my imprisonment.

Will History Lie?

History will associate my name as one of the participators in the crime, but in doing so it will lie, as I was as guiltless as an unborn babe as to knowledge or connection in any way whatsoever in the horrible crime. When Gen. Thomas Ewing,[4] who had been retained by me as counsel, came to see me in my cell he remarked that he would have nothing to do with the case if I was in any way connected with the crime. I told him that I was as innocent as he was himself as to knowledge, connection or participation therein; that had I been a party to it, or have counseled, abetted or aided in any manner the commission of the horrible act, I would have scorned to solicit defense; would have pleaded guilty to the charge and met with whatever doom the government might impose with as much fortitude as I could command, feeling that I had by my own act entailed upon myself its full burden and merit.

After the consultation had ended he became counsel for me. I narrated to him the entire knowledge I possessed, and my connection with Booth at one time, and gave the names of witnesses to be summoned in my case. As he was upon the point of leaving my cell his eye centered upon the hood, which had been removed before his entry and hurriedly thrown into one corner of the cell. He inquired of me what it was, and I remarked, handing it to him, "A torture invented by Edwin M. Stanton, secretary of war."

After a careful examination of it in all its devices and details he made some very uncomplimentary remarks in reference to Stanton, which I forbear expressing.[5] I requested him in the opening of my defense to give the nation and the world at large my treatment. His reply, in part, was: "The less you say about that, the better; you have a d--- hard court to try you."[6]

Hope died within my heart at his utterances, and from that hour I endeavored to nerve myself to meet my fate, fully expecting to meet with death. To my father, who was allowed to see me twice during my trial,[7] I expressed the same views, stating that perjury was being resorted to secure my conviction.

From the moment General Ewing made that remark I lost all interest in the trial and surroundings, and patiently awaited my doom --- death, I thought.

Chapter Sixteen

—

EPILOGUE

—

No Connection to Confederate Authorities---Herold Was But a Boy---Only Four Concerned with Murder---Those Cipher Letters---Arnold Compared to Dreyfus---He Received No Sympathy---Arnold's Present Home---A Typographical Error.

[Saturday, December 20, 1902]

There never was any connection between Booth and the Confederate authorities. I was in Booth's confidence, and had anything existed as such he would have made known the fact to me. Besides, such a quixotic scheme would have been laughed at by them had it been possible for Booth to have obtained audience with them, and he would have been dismissed from their presence, and in all probability been overlooked as an insane man. The scheme originated in Booth's own visionary mind; he became a monomaniac on the success of the Confederate arms, a condition which generally follows when a man's thoughts are constantly centered upon one subject alone.

His last act was the act of a madman, and I am convinced that he did it in a moment of temporary insanity, caused by the defeat of the Confederate armies, and the cause so dear to his heart lost. This is my opinion, which cannot be controverted in this world; its truth or falsity will only be known in the world to come.

The men by whom he had been surrounded and who had associated themselves with him were, to a great extent, ignorant men. They clung to him for the bounty they were receiving at Booth's hand. No labor to perform to earn their living, Booth providing it, and they were willing to let it so continue, hugging within themselves the thought the fast-approaching end of the war would soon dissolve companionship and terminate the conspiracy in which they were engaged, without any bodily harm falling to their lot.

When, in his frenzy, he made known his design to them they were so entangled that retreat was impossible, and even had they attempted to do so, without surrendering themselves to the authorities, their knowledge alone would have made them just as guilty before the law as if the blow had been struck by their own hand.

Herold Was But a Boy.

Herold, a mere boy, acting in the role of pilot, steering Booth through the country, taking no part in the murder itself, thought, in his ignorance of the law, that he would not be reached. Atzerodt, of same mold, thought the same when he fled, failing to execute the part assigned him to be performed by Booth, ignorant of the fact that before the law he was just as guilty as Booth, who committed the deed.[1]

Payne was differently situated. He was far from his native state in a strange city -- penniless. Booth had for months provided for him -- food, lodging and raiment, and limited means to meet his daily incidental expenses. For all these things he could not be ungrateful; besides, he was subordinate to Booth's stronger mind, who controlled him in his every movement, and when the crime to be committed was sprung upon him he was as bold and fearless as Booth himself, and tried his best to carry on the part allotted to him by Booth to perform.

Only Four Concerned.

These four men comprised the entire conspirators in that crime. No knowledge of it extended beyond them; according to confessions made by Herold and Atzerodt, it was first made known at 8 o'clock and executed at 10 o'clock the same evening.[2]

No officials of the Confederate government had any knowledge in regard to it, although it was attempted to be shown by the military commission that they had, through many witnesses.[3] Everything went upon our trial. It was fixed in its entirety, and all were condemned before being heard. No cross-examination of witnesses, their evidence being so deep laid that no opening was left, besides counsel declined to do so, having no groundwork left to stand upon, and so that long-drawn-out trial, lasting months, daily adding to the public excitement, grew from a mere molehill to a stupendous structure, reared and built through perjury.[4]

There was a witness to establish the conspiracy from Baltimore, named William Spandauer, who finally died in the Maryland Penitentiary. When counsel desired that he be produced for cross-examination he was nowhere to be found; he had been spirited away by the prosecution, not, however, before leaving his imprint before the court.[5]

Those Cipher Letters.

Cipher letters were found floating in the water at Moorhead City, N.C., unblurred by contact with the water, intended no doubt to encircle me at Fortress Monroe with participation in the crime; in fact, the conspiracy through the government witnesses grew to immense proportions, extending from the Lakes to the Gulf, even penetrating into Canada, whereas, it was but the act of four deluded men, dwelling in the City of Washington.

Retribution has followed in the wake of that trial. Numerous, not very important, witnesses died during my incarceration. Soon after the verdict some died from suicide, and later on some died in the penitentiary, while some served terms in the penitentiary.[6] Of the members of the court who sat in condemnation of me I am not advised, but the prosecuting judge advocate and his assistants, I think, have been called before the bar of God.[7]

Compared to Dreyfus.

The late Dreyfus trial in France was a counterpart in many respects to my own; the same means employed and resorted to convict -- viz., forged documentary evidence, as well as false swearing -- the same arm of the government service sitting in judgment. But I will say for France that when the prisoner appeared and stood before the military court he stood as a man, as a guiltless man, not as a condemned convict and felon weighed down in shackles and chains; neither was he tortured before and during his trial, and was publicly degraded only after conviction.

This miscarriage of justice in his case aroused the public of all nations in Europe, and also the public of the United States. The official organs, however, representing the governments abroad, as well as my own remained in passive silence, that no offense should be given to the nations on friendly terms, or that any breach of international law should occur. At the same time every nation in Europe, as well as the United States, had been guilty of the very same thing which was condemned by the press of the civilized world.

The sentence inflicted upon Dreyfus was loudly condemned far and near as a miscarriage of justice, and the stress upon the president of the French Republic became so great that a pardon was granted Dreyfus. The crime of which he was accused was false in every particular in case, his only "offense" being that he was a Jew.

Received No Sympathy.

In my case, far worse conducted than in Dreyfus' case, I have yet to learn or hear of a single voice raised in my behalf, or denouncing my treatment, but, to the contrary, correspondents of the press, at times, contributed scurrilous articles against me, in which no truth exists, their hatred not satiated although 30 years have elapsed.

Age is creeping upon me, I am steadily marching toward that goal where many have gone before me, and before many years have passed will reach it, and there confront my accusers, and then, and not until then, will the mysteries surrounding my unjust trial, torture and condemnation be truthfully revealed.

                              SAMUEL BLAND ARNOLD.

Arnold's Present Home.

Mr. Arnold lived in Baltimore from time to time up until about six years ago, when he decided to seek the peace and quiet of a country life. Since that time he has been residing on a farm near Friendship, Anne Arundel County, coming to Baltimore at infrequent periods.[8] About twice each year he comes to Baltimore and spends some days at the home of his brother, Mr. Charles A. Arnold, at the corner of the York Road and Chestnut Hill Avenue. Mr. Arnold during his residence in Baltimore, had always been looked upon by those who came in contact with him as a man of most retiring disposition, and was ever exceedingly loath to speak of the great tragedy or its surrounding circumstances that had come to wreck his entire life.

In all those years of his life Mr. Arnold was undoubtedly what he has described himself -- a misanthropist. On the farm in Anne Arundel county he has sought a seclusion and quiet free from the busy haunts of man, which he could not find in a big city. Even in his immediate locality in the country he is simply known as Mr. Arnold, and but few, if any, know that in this old man has been locked the story of one of the greatest tragedies of life.

In striking contrast with the once-powerful frame and fiery spirit of youth, this wrinkled old man, with head and beard whitened by the passage of nearly 70 years, awaits the sounding of the last trumpet. A self-created hermit from the ordinary friendships and courtesies of mankind, he is beloved by the brute creation.

Samuel B. Arnold at Friendship, 1902

In his dogs, his pigeons, his chickens and the animals of the farm is his greatest pleasure centered, and all of these dumb creatures acknowledge him as a friend. In these friends of the farm, filled in occasionally by visits of relatives in Baltimore, does Samuel Bland Arnold find the consolation of his declining days.

A Typographical Error.

Note. -- Mr. Arnold, in a communication to The *American*, calls attention to a typographical error in that portion of the serial published on Thursday, December 11. In writing his original manuscript in that portion dealing with his arrest, Mr. Arnold, after telling of the arrival of the detectives and the presenting by them of a letter from his father, advising him to tell anything that he might happen to know about the matter, stated: "After perusing it, the detectives asked whether I intended to comply with the request of my father. I stated yes, and told them that I knew nothing concerning it, nor was I at the time in any manner connected with Booth or others." The latter sentence was published so as to read: "I stated yes, and told them that I knew nothing concerning it, nor was I at any time, in any manner connected with Booth or others."

In calling attention to the unintentional substitution of the word "any" for "the" in the sentence, which changed its meaning, Mr. Arnold says:

"I find that I have been misquoted, or it may be a typographical error. In fact, it is evidence against me not contained either in my manuscript or upon the records, as far as I can remember, of the proceedings before that military court. I have plainly stated that when I first engaged with Booth in his scheme I informed my family that I was employed by him in the oil business. This was said to remove any suspicion in their minds. All my family were totally ignorant of the whole affair. Again, as you have narrated, when it was learned that John Wilkes Booth was the hand that struck the fatal blow it startled me. I felt assured that my former connection and intimacy with Booth would lead to my arrest, etc., and had I been differently situated I would have surrendered myself (in my entire innocence) into the hands of the government.

"With the above and with the fact of my having received a letter from my father, in which he seemed to think I was in some way connected with it, would have of itself prevented me denying that which you have stated --- viz.: that I told the detectives that I knew nothing of it (this may be correct), but that I denied or said, as you have published, `nor was I at any time, in any manner connected with Booth or others,' is a flat contradiction of avowed utterances related above, I denied nothing. I told the truth then; I proclaim it now. I hid nothing --- my innocence I wished to establish --- and the government had the paper, and by the arrest of others supposed to be implicated, they could either affirm or deny the accuracy of its contents."

THE END.

Appendix A
—

ARNOLD'S FIRST STATEMENT
—

The following statement was written by Sam Arnold in the Baltimore office of Provost Marshal James L. McPhail. Soon after Arnold's arrest, the Baltimore papers got word that the prisoner intended to make a statement, and their reporting of this fact led Secretary of War Stanton to reprimand McPhail in the sharpest terms. As it happened, the news was not leaked through McPhail, but through John Potts, Chief Clerk of the War Department, who accompanied Arnold and the detectives back to Baltimore from Fortress Monroe.[1]

A manuscript copy of original document is in the National Archives, Record Group 94, Records of the Advocate General's Office. It is available on Microcopy M-619, Reel 458, Frames 305-312. It is copied here precisely as it appeared in the records. The statement was published in the *Baltimore American* on January 18, 1869.

Baltimore,   186

To whom it may concern

Know that I Saml B Arnold, about the latter part of August or first part of September, 1864, was sent for by J. Wilkes Booth, who was a guest at Barnum Hotel City of Baltimore Md. to come to see him. Had not seen the same J Wilkes Booth since 1852, when we both were schoolmates together at St Timothy's Hall President L Van Bokelin then having said Hall as place of tuition. Reception warm calling for wine and cigars conversing a short time upon our former School boy days we were interrupted by a knock at the door when Michael O. Loughlin was ushered in. After a formal introduction we sat sipping our wine, and then smoke a cigar.

During smoking he having heard previously of my feelings or sentiments, he spoke in glowing terms of the Confederacy and of the number of surplus prisoners in the hands of the United States, and then issued the proposition by J Wilkes Booth and which he J Wilkes Booth thought could be accomplished viz: Kidnapping President Lincoln as he frequently went unguarded out to Soldiers Home, and he thought he could be picked up carried to Richmond, and for his exchange produce the exchange (for the President) of all the prisoners in the Federal Hands. He J Wilkes Booth the originator asked if we would enter into it, after the painting of the chance of success in such glowing colors, we consented viz: Michael O Loughlin and myself, secrecy bound not to divulge it to a living soul, saw him no more. Yes I saw him again and then he J Wilkes Booth left to arrange the business north. First to New York then to the Oil regions, from there to Boston and finally to Canada. was to be back in a month. Received a letter which I destroyed stating he was laid up with Eryeocippolis in the arm and as soon as he was able, he would be with us. Months rolled around, he did not make his appearance until sometime in January. In his trunk he had two guns (maker unknown) Cap, Cartridges which were placed in the Gun Stock, (Spencer Rifles, I think called) Revolver Knife bells cartridge Boses cartridge Caps Canteen. All fully fixed out, which were to be used in case of pursuit, and two pieces handcuffs to handcuff the President. His trunk being so heavy he gave the Pistols knives and handcuffs Michael O. Loughlin and myself to have shipped or bring to Washington, to which place he had gone, bought Horse Buggy Wagon and harness leaving the team +c to drive on to Washington. Started from Baltimore about twelve or One O'clock, after having shipped the Box containing the Knives Handcuffs and pistols, arriving in Washington at seven or half past seven. Met him on the street as we were passing theatre, we alighted took a drink and he told us of the Theatre plan slightly saying he would wait till we put the Horse away and tell us more fully, he had previously as I now remember spoken of the chance in the Theatre if we could not succeed in the other at Soldiers Home. We went to Theatre that night he J Wilkes Booth telling us about the different back entrances and how feasible the plan was He J Wilkes Booth had rented a Stable in rear of the Theatre having bought two Horses down in the country, one in stable behind Theatre, the other at livery. Met him next day went to Breakfast together, he was always pressed with business with a man unknown and then only by name John Surratt. Most of Booths time was spent with him, we were left entirely in the dark. Michael O. Loughlin and myself rented a room in D Street 420 No. obtained meals at Franklin House cor of 8th and D St. and there lived for nearly two months, seeing him perhaps thrice or four times per week and when seen always but a short time still pressing business always on hand, viz: John Surrat Michael O Loughlin and myself drove out occasionally the Horse liveried at Nailors Stable drove always (but once) in the City and Georgetown, the once excepted across Eastern Branch Bridge when we went upwards of five miles and returned I suppose. That was the only time I ever went over the Bridge. How often J Wilkes Booth crossed I cannot state, but from his own words often. There was Michael O Loughlin time spent and mine for the most part down at Rullman's Hotel and Leecheaw House on Pennsylvania ------ and Louisiana Avenues in drinking and amusements with others Baltimoreans besides ourselves.

Congregating there all of whom knew nothing of our business but selling oil stock Oil stock was the blind for them as well as my family. During the latter part of March while standing on Rullmans and Leecheaus Porch between 11 + 12 O'clock P M, a young man name unknown, as I cannot remember names about 5 feet 5 or 6 ins high thick set, long nose, sharp chin, wide cheek, small eye, I think grey, dark hair and well dressed, color dont remember said called Michael O Loughlin aside and said J Wilkes Booth wish to see us both at Gothers Saloon on Avenue. I was there for the first time introduced to him, but forget his name We walked up together. Michael O. Loughlin this unknown and myself were ushered into the presence of J Wilkes Booth who introduced me to John Surrat, Atzrodt ("alias") Port Tobacco ("alias") Mosby making in all seven persons J Wilkes Booth had stated to Michael O. Loughlin, to bring me up in good humor (still always in the dark) Then commenced the plan

Each had his part to perform first I was to rush in the Box and seize the President whilst Atzrodt "alias" Port Tobacco and J Wilkes Booth were to handcuff him and lower him on the stage whilst Mosby was to catch him and hold him untill we all got down. Surrat and unknown to be on the other side of Bridge to facilitate escape, afterwards changed to Mosby and Booth to catch him in Box throw him down to me on Stage. O Loughlin and unknown to put gas out, Surrat, Atzrodt "alias" Port Tobacco to be on the other side of Bridge. I was opposed to the whole proceeding, said it could not be done or accomplished if even which was of itself an impossibility to get him out of the Box and to the Bridge we would be stopped by sentinel. Shoot the sentinel says Booth, I said that would not do for if an alarm was given then the whole thing was up. as for me I wanted a Shadow of a chance M. O Loughlin wanted to argue the same thing whereupon J Wilkes Booth remarked you find fault with every thing concerned about it. I said no I wanted to have a chance and I intended to have it, that he could be the leader of the party but not my executioner whereupon J Wilkes Booth remarked in a stern commanding and angry voice, do you know you are liable to be shot your oath, I told him the plan a basis had been changed and a compact broken, on the part of one is broken by all. If you feel inclined to shoot me, you have no further to go I shall defend myself. This if I remember arightly was on a Thursday or Friday night when I said Gentlemen if this is not accomplished this week I forever withdraw from it, staid up till about 6 or 7 O'clock A.M. Friday or Saturday and then to bed remained in doors till twelve. I arose and went to get my breakfast. M. O. Loughlin and myself room together both arose at the same time and were always together in a measure, about two or three O'clock J Wilkes Booth called at Leechaus House to see O. Loughlin. What passed I know not. I told him I wanted to see him, Says he speak out, well John what I said last night, I mean if not done this week I withdraw. Went to bed about 7 1/2 O'clock P.M. next day Was to be accomplished on the 7th St. road, it failed Sunday.

I staid in Washington and Monday or Tuesday I returned to the City of Baltimore and thence to Hookstown. J Wilkes Booth in mean time went to New York and returned during week. Saturday I think said he wished to see me on very urgent business. Father sent for me. I came from Country, and he had gone to Washington, whereupon I wrote him the letter published, Richmond authorities as far as I know knew nothing on the Conspiracy. The letter was written after my return to Country, after finding he could not wait to see me in Baltimore. During week I came in City again, met M. O. Loughlin, who asked me to go to Washington to finally arrange his affairs. I went in the morning Friday returning same day, cut loose forever from it. Received a letter J H Wharton at Fort Monroe giving me employment. Went to Country got my clothing and Saturday first day of April left Baltimore for Fort Monroe at which place I have remained never corresponding with Booth or seeing him from above named date the present writing. The ground work was to kidnap the President without any violence none others were included therein. He never to me said he would kill him, further than this I know nothing and am innocent of having taken any part whatever in the dark deed committed.

The plan of escape Was place Mr Lincoln in the buggy purchased for that purpose cross Eastern Branch Bridge. Surrat and Atzrodt "alias" Port Tobacco to Pilot them to where a boat was concealed, turn Horses loose, place the President in the boat and cross the Potomac to Virginia Shore and thence to make our way to Richmond Surrat knew the route and was to act as Pilot.

A Box painted black like into a sword box was sent to Booth from Hotel by a Porter there, to our room, next day transfered in wagon. O Loughlin acting Pilot to some place. I was not present after giving box to driver went to Georgetown and O Loughlin had the full charge of it. M O Loughlin said he took it to a Mr. Heard and from thence the unknown carried it to his Horse, took guns out and carried then to Peedee[2]. This latter clause Booth told me.

(Signed) Saml. B. Arnold

Baltimore April 18th 1865.

Witness V Randall
        E. G. Horner

The aforegoing confession of Saml. B. Arnold, whose name is attached thereto, was made in his hand writing and acknowledged by him to be his free act and deed and given into my hands and I had it witnessed as above. William McPhail.

Appendix B

—

THE WILKES BOOTH CONSPIRACY

—

Letter From Arnold to His Mother

————

Doylestown (Pa.) Democrat, July 27, 1867

*Clipping in the Lincoln Obsequies
Scrapbook
Library of Congress*

—

The following letter from Arnold, one of the conspirators sentenced to imprisonment for life, written to his mother the night before the execution of Harold, Payne, Atzerodt, and Mrs. Surratt, has never been published. Its genuineness cannot be doubted. It was handed by Arnold to Colonel Fredericks, on duty at the Arsenal, to be given to his mother after his removal to the Dry Tortugas, which was done, but not until a copy had been made. The copy Colonel Fredericks gave to Dr. O'Neal, of Gettysburg, which the latter loaned to the editor of *The Democrat*, on his late visit to that place, for the purpose of publication.

My Dear, Dear Mother --- For some time, perhaps forever, these are the last lines that ever the hand of your loved, and ever loving son shall be transcribed upon paper to you. Be cheerful, be comforted under your present affliction; for your care feel that the brow which oft in infancy your breath has fanned, as you lulled me to sleep upon your bosom, still retains its former innocence, even though doomed to prison as a common felon. That the nutriment obtained from your breast instilled qualities within me that I can proudly toast are unequalled by man; and not of blood but human kindness; and my honored name sustains its former lustre; nor does my conscience upbraid me for any act ever committed against my fellow man. All who knew me loved me, even black and white, and none can ever reproach me even as having committed an ungentlemanly act, nor having ever seen me do or speak a malicious thing; all who know me know 'tis truth I write. "Nihil Desparandum." While there's life there's hope. We may yet be united, if not on earth assuredly in heaven. Even while connected with the abduction scheme I was the most miserable being on earth. 'Twas a cankering sore within my heart, and daily was consuming my very vitals, to think that I, who was always open in my actions, was practicing deceit, especially towards those whose whole hearts would have gratified my every wish --- my family. I shunned conversation, etc., kept aloof from you all, for I did not wish that the grief and marks of trouble depicted on my brow should give you a moment's pain. Had I followed your early teachings of infancy, the moral culture of youth and the example set before me in manhood, I, that never was ordained by God to fill my present position, would today be at liberty, still an honor, a solace, a prop, to you and father in your old days. But in an evil hour I was tempted from the path of virtue and rectitude, and by no act or knowledge (for which I was a party to, viz., abduction was conceived and died unborn), of mine, but by the cowardly act of a dishonored wretch, coward at heart, who had no soul, I am doomed to fill a place amid a throng of criminals. Yet I will retain all my former qualities, and shall not be contaminated thereby. That which all the vices of the world and mankind could not make, by one fell stroke, an assassin tried to make me; but his murderous intent was frustrated by my country; yet they have clothed me in a felon's garb, but, thank God, have not made me a felon. No matter how situated or placed, I will ever be my former self --- a soul the embodiment of truth, honor, innocence and purity --- and am today, within my narrow cell, one of the "noblest works of God," "an honest and truthful man."

Dear Mother, God be my witness, I know nothing of the fact or act for which I suffer, and you and whoever knew me, I feel, are satisfied of the fact. Remember me to all my friends, for I had many, and especially she, of all others, who has been a second mother to me, in advice, interest in my welfare, and kindness, affection, and love --- Mrs. Garner --- and tell her let not the present misfortune cause the leaf to wither, but let it ever be kept a green and flourishing plant within her memory, and he, whom none loved better than I, her son Bob.[1] Ever remember me as I was, have been, and still am to him. My family and her family, in my affections, are twins. During my imprisonment I shall ever feel grateful for the kind treatment and many acts of kindness of those who have had me in charge. They shall be closeted with the many scenes of the happy past within my memory, from the highest command to the lowest, viz., --- Gen. J.F. Hartranft, Col. W.H.H. McCall, Col. Frederick, Col. Dodd, and last, though not least, W.R. Kenny, the sergeant of the call. No token to leave any but good will and gratitude. Remember each and honor all for their kindness to your unfortunate son. In thus parting and writing to you, it causes my placid and resigned feelings to burst their merements [?], and the tear starts unbidden from an overflowing heart. I am not lost. I still am human. Farewells where forever should be sudden. Goodbye. God bless you all, guide, instruct and save you. Be not heartsick, we will meet again, if not on earth, in eternity.

Your devoted and loving son,
SAMUEL B. ARNOLD.

N.B. Keep my dog till he dies. For my sake let him be treated well, and when dead bury him. Erect a slab inscription, "A true friend," for he would never forsake me even should the whole world do so. He loved me, even the ground I walked upon, and I loved him. Poor Dash! We have forever parted. Thou without a soul, yet did you love me, and thou art not forgotten.

Appendix C

—

DEATH OF ARNOLD THE CONSPIRATOR

—

MAN WHO PLANNED TO ABDUCT PRESIDENT LINCOLN

—

CLOSE OF A TRAGIC CAREER

—

Consumption Claims Aged Man at Home of Relative, in Waverly.

—

Was Arrested, With Others, Immediately After the Death of the President and Sentenced to Dry Tortugas -- American Published Confession in 1902 in Which He Denied All Knowledge of Any Except Kidnapping Plot.

Baltimore American, September 22, 1906

Samuel Bland Arnold, one of the Lincoln Conspirators, and who in the last years of his life stoutly maintained that injustice had been done to many of those who were caught in the government dragnet following the murder of the great war president, died yesterday afternoon at 2:45 o'clock at the home of Mrs. Helen T. Arnold, a sister-in-law, living at 633 Madison

Street, Waverly.[1]

Mr. Arnold celebrated his seventy-second birthday on September 6 last. His death was due to consumption, of which he had been a sufferer for only a short time.

On Tuesday last he was paralyzed and lost the power of speech. He was unconscious when he died. He made no reference to the Lincoln conspiracy to his relatives in late years.

Mr. Arnold had lived in seclusion on his farm, near Fair Haven, in Anne Arundel county, for years. He had fairly good health up to about two years ago, when he fell and fractured a bone in his hip. The fracture was reduced at the Hopkins Hospital. Mr. Arnold began to fail after that. He could not move about his farm with the same freedom he had enjoyed previously, and he spent nearly all his time with his chickens and dogs.

About two months ago he came to Baltimore and went to the home of his sister-in-law, Mrs. Helen T.H. Arnold. He complained of feeling unwell, and he was placed in the care of a physician. His condition was described as galloping consumption, and no hopes were held out for his recovery.

Approach of End.

On Monday he grew rapidly worse, and his sister, Mrs. Oregon Jackson,[2] of Washington, was sent for. She, with Mrs. Arnold and her daughter and son, was at his bedside when death came.

The funeral of this man, who figured in one of the greatest tragedies in the history of the nation, will take place on Monday afternoon at 2 o'clock. It will be simple and plain, as was his life. He was a Methodist, and a minister of that faith will say a prayer at the house of Mrs. Arnold, on Madison street, and there will be prayers in Greenmount, where interment will take place.

It is at Greenmount that John Wilkes Booth, the assassin of Lincoln, is buried, along with the other members of the distinguished Booth family.[3]

Mr. Arnold is supposed to have left some property. Mrs. Jackson, his sister, stated last night that Mr. Arnold had long cherished the hope of publishing a book bearing on the Lincoln conspiracy. He had all his data in hand and had even gone so far as to engage a publisher in Washington to take up the work.

The strong, clear-cut features of Mr. Arnold did not seem last night to have suffered much through the ravages of time. He very much resembles the pictures taken of him a quarter of a century ago, wearing, as he did then, a mustache and gotee.

A Romantic Life.

The life story of Samuel Bland Arnold is one of graphic interest. Immediately following the assassination of President Lincoln the name of Arnold, with that of his fellow-conspirators, was on almost every tongue, and, while for years following the conviction of Arnold and his sentence to Dry Tortugas he figured almost constantly in the newspapers, yet it was not until December of 1902 that what he said was the true story of his connection with the conspiracy was given to the public.

In the latter part of 1902 the *American* learned that Arnold had prepared a story of his life in diary form covering more than 40,000 words, and that he had steadfastly refused to allow this to be given out until after his death.

After considerable correspondence with Mr. Arnold, coupled with the persuasion of relatives, who desired his vindication on the assassination charge while yet he lived, Mr. Arnold finally consented to allow The *American* to publish his story.

The recital was given to the public in serial form from Sunday, December 7, 1902 to Saturday, December 20, following and created widespread interest and comment. By a special arrangement with The *American* such papers as the *New York Sun*, the *Atlanta Constitution, Chicago Tribune, Louisville Courier-Journal* and about 30 other of the most representative newspapers of the country published the story simultaneously.

A Remarkable Story.

It was a remarkable story that the manuscript of Samuel B. Arnold unfolded -- a story of plots to capture the chief executive of the nation and convey him within the Confederate lines, conceived under the supposed impulses of patriotism to the South; of passions stirred to the depth of human souls as nothing but the impulses of hearts embittered by civil strife could engender, and of imprisonment, cruelty and torture.

"It has not been written through malice or vindictiveness; I have confined myself to the truth," said Arnold, after a recitation of circumstances which, in days of internal peace, prosperity and happiness, when the last traces of the bitterness of war have been swept aside forever, read like the revelation of some horrible nightmare, impossible of a reality.

An autobiographical recitation of wrongs by a man who could never forget, a man who sought seclusion and avoided his fellow-men, a misanthropist by his own statement, The *American* presented his life story upon its own basis; a public unprejudiced and unbiased to sit in judgment upon its statements.

"The burnt child dreads the fire," wrote Arnold, and in his misanthropic feelings a hatred of mankind, conceived and fostered in a contact with the stern arm of military law, he had intended to let his story slumber until he himself had passed into the great unknown, when he thought that conditions might be ripe for the reception of his recital.

Plots That Failed.

The manuscript of Arnold, in relation to its preparation, extended over a long period of years. That portion in which a most interesting account was given of the inception of the plots to kidnap President Lincoln, with their successive failures and the reasons therefor, giving names, dates and locations connected therewith, was written in the year 1867, while Arnold was confined in the Dry Tortugas, Florida, and attested to before a notary public and a special commissioner appointed by the Congressional Commission to investigate into the circumstances surrounding the assassination of the president. A second portion of the same document gave a succession of questions put to Arnold as to his life, etc., by the notary public.

At that time the writings stopped for many years, but in the early nineties Mr. Arnold began the task of writing the entire story of his life. With painstaking efforts he placed in black and white a graphic story, dealing with the entire subject at hand, and recorded events that to the mind of the present seem too terrible to be real.

Of the eight men who, according to the story of Arnold, conspired together to abduct President Lincoln, but one now lives, Mr. John H. Surratt, who now resides in this city. Mr. Surratt is the son of Mrs. Mary E. Surratt, who was one of those hanged in the arsenal at Washington for the murder of the martyred president, and who is now generally looked upon as having been innocent of the crime for which she suffered the death penalty.

John Wilkes Booth, the actual murderer of Lincoln, was shot and killed when captured in a barn in Northern Virginia. David E. Herold, who was captured with him, and Lewis Payne and George A. Atzerodt, went to their death on the scaffold with Mrs. Surratt. Samuel B. Arnold, Dr. Samuel A. Mudd, Michael O'Laughlin and Edward Spangler were tried for the murder of the president with the others, and were sentenced to life imprisonment in the Dry Tortugas. Arnold was the last of these latter men, all of whom were pardoned by President Johnson in 1869.

Surratt Escaped.

Surratt, the only other living conspirator, according to the story of Arnold, fled the country after the assassination of President Lincoln. Surratt was in Elmira, N.Y., when the assassination took place, and he vanished from sight in spite of the utmost endeavors of government detectives to arrest him, and was not heard of again for two years. He was later arrested abroad. The two years which had elapsed since his flight had calmed down public indignation, and he was neither executed nor had to suffer the same punishment as those of his alleged confederates, who were sent to the Dry Tortugas.

That Arnold had no part in the actual assassination, he having left Washington sometime previous, and having been employed at Old Point Comfort as a clerk, when that great crime was committed, has long since received practical acknowledgement at the hands of the public, and in his statement given out he told what he said was the entire story of the affair as far as his knowledge extended. Knowledge of a plan to assassinate President Lincoln he confined to Booth, Payne, Atzerodt and Herold, and held Mrs. Surratt as entirely guiltless of the crime of which she was charged, and for which she suffered the death penalty.

"The Dry Tortugas a Hell."

Probably the most remarkable portion of the story of Arnold, as told by himself, was the recital of cruelties practiced upon himself and other prisoners of the government, as well as to soldiers themselves at the Dry Tortugas, which he described as a veritable hell on earth. These events, he said, he recorded from day to day in a diary, from which his manuscript in full was compiled.

Arnold's arrest was brought about by the circumstance of the finding of a letter in the trunk of John Wilkes Booth, after the assassination, of which Arnold spoke at length in his manuscript. While at the time this letter was seized upon by the prosecution as strong evidence against Arnold, it was later regarded as supporting his claim that his part alone was in the conspiracy to abduct Lincoln, and that he had even practically abandoned the idea of this, and that the letter was intended to dissuade Booth from that scheme.

Approval of Sentence.

When the commission found Arnold guilty he was

sentenced to imprisonment at hard labor for life, at such place as the President should direct. President Johnson approved the findings of the commission in regard to the execution of Herold, Atzerodt, Payne and Mrs. Surratt, and of imprisonment for the others in the following words:

"The foregoing sentences in the cases of David E. Herold, G.A. Atzerodt, Lewis Payne, Michael O'Laughlin, Edward Spangler, Samuel Arnold, Mary E. Surratt and Samuel A. Mudd are hereby approved, and it is ordered that the sentences of said David E. Herold, G.A. Atzerodt, Lewis Payne and Mary E. Surratt be carried into execution by the proper military authority, under the direction of the secretary of war, on the 7th day of July, 1865, between the hours of 10 o'clock A.M. and 2 o'clock P.M. of that day. It is further ordered that the prisoners Samuel Arnold, Samuel A. Mudd, Edward Spangler and Michael O'Laughlin be confined at hard labor in the penitentiary at Albany, N.Y., during the period designated in their respective sentences."

The above approval was made on July 5, 1865, and 10 days later President Johnson modified the order so that the prisoners be confined at the Dry Tortugas instead of at the Albany Penitentiary.

"Unspeakable Cruelties."

It was this change from Albany to Dry Tortugas that opened the way for what Arnold claimed were unspeakable cruelties. His statement given out in 1902 went into the most minute details of what happened on the island off the Florida coast.

With the use of names of officers of the United States Army and of soldiers under them, Arnold told harrowing stories of how prisoners on the island were made to carry heavy cannon balls in circles under a tropical sun until they dropped with fatigue; how men were thrown into the sea with shot tied to their feet; how they were placed in casemates covered with slime and moisture and a prey to reptiles and vermin, and how other almost unspeakable cruelties and indignities were heaped upon them.

With a like use of names and dates Arnold told how soldiers were given similar inhumane treatment by their officers for the slightest infraction of regulations. He told, also, how prisoners were shot down without provocation, and how the soldiers themselves were not only ready to aid prisoners to escape in many instances, but took long chances of starvation at sea themselves to escape what Arnold termed the "Hells of

Tortugas."

He gave a graphic, yet sickening, account of scenes of horror that followed the advent of yellow fever. His story, as stated, was not only a circumstantial one, but one which contained numerous official documents, to which he gained access while serving as clerk under military commanders on the island.

Kidnapping Plot.

In the part of Arnold's confession concerning the plot to kidnap Lincoln, he said that he first discussed the subject with Wilkes Booth in September, 1864, at Barnum's Hotel, in Baltimore. The plan hatched at that time by Booth, O'Laughlin and himself was to capture the President when he went to visit the Soldiers' Home, and to carry him across the Potomac and to convey him to Richmond.

In his story at this point Arnold told of going to Washington with the purpose of carrying out the abduction scheme. The events which followed are best told by Arnold's own confession, as follows:

"The President having ceased visiting the Soldiers' Home, Booth proposed a plan to abduct him from the theater by carrying him back off the stage by the back entrance, place him in a buggy which he was to have in attendance, and during the confusion which would be produced by the turning off of the gas, make good our escape. I objected to any such arrangement, and plainly pointed out its utter impracticability, and told Booth it could not be accomplished. He would listen to no argument I could bring forth, and seemed resolved in carrying out this mad scheme. He endeavored to obtain a man from New York to turn off the gas. In this he failed -- so he informed me.

"This was in the latter part of January or the early part of February, 1865, Booth at this time was stopping at the National Hotel. About this time I called at his room, accompanied by O'Laughlin, and, upon entering, was introduced to Surratt under the name, I think, of Cole. This was about 10 or 11 o'clock in the morning, and Booth was still in bed. This was the first time I ever met Surratt. Surratt left a few moments after we came in, and Booth informed us that he was one of the parties engaged in the abduction, and that his name was Surratt.

A Mother's Dreams.

"About this time Booth told me he had received a letter

from his mother, in which she stated that she had fearful dreams about him. She sent his brother, Junius Brutus, to Washington to persuade him to come home, so Booth told me. Booth told me that he did not wish his brother to know how many horses he had, as he knew that his brother would ask for an explanation as to why he kept so many. He asked me then to go down to Cleaver's stable, and I did so. He told Mr. Cleaver that I had purchased the horse, and he was turned over to me.

"About a week afterward I went to the stable, paid the livery on the horse and rode him up to the corner of D and Eighth streets and turned him over either to O'Laughlin or Booth. I never saw the horse afterwards. Booth afterwards repaid me for the board of the horse.

"Booth was absent from the city of Washington for the best part of the month of February. On his return he stated that he had been to New York. On the night of March 15, 1865, about 12 or 12:30 o'clock, O'Laughlin and myself were about leaving Rullman's Hotel, on our way to our room, when Booth sent a messenger (Herold), who at that time was unknown to me, requesting us to accompany Herold to Gotier's Eating Saloon. (Herold, I learned from O'Laughlin, had been introduced to him that day by Booth during their buggy ride.)

"We, accordingly, went up and were ushered into the room, where, seated around a table, were Booth, Surratt, Atzerodt, alias Port Tobacco, and Payne, alias Mosby, all of whom, with the exception of Booth and Surratt, I had never seen nor heard of before. We were then formally introduced. Oysters, liquors and cigars were obtained. Booth then remarked that those gathered were the parties engaged to assist in the abduction of the president. The plan of abducting him from the theater was then introduced and discoursed upon, Booth saying that if it could not be done from the lower box it could from the upper one.

The Parts Allotted.

"He set forth the part he wished each one to perform. He and Payne, alias Mosby, were to seize the president in the box, O'Laughlin and Herold to put out the gas; I was to jump upon the stage and assist them as he was lowered down from the box, and Surratt and Atzerodt, alias Port Tobacco, were to be on the other side of the Eastern Branch bridge to act as pilots and to assist in conveying him to the boats which had been purchased by Booth. Booth said everything was in readiness.

"The gist of the conversation during the meeting was as to whether it could or could not be accomplished in the manner proposed. After listening to Booth and the others, I firmly protested and objected to the whole scheme, and told them of its utter impracticability. I stated that prisoners were being exchanged and that the object of the abduction had been accomplished; that patriotism was the motive that prompted me in joining the scheme, not ambition, and that I wanted a shadow of a chance for my life and that I intended having it.

"Then an angry discussion arose between Booth and myself, in which he threatened to shoot me. I told him that two could play at that game, and before them all expressed my firm determination to have nothing more to do with it after that week. About 5 o'clock in the morning the meeting broke up and O'Laughlin and myself went to our room at Mrs. Van Tynes.

"The next day, as I was standing in front of Rullman's Hotel, Pennsylvania avenue, in company with O'Laughlin, Booth came riding by on horseback and stopped and called O'Laughlin. He conversed with him a short time, and then O'Laughlin returned, saying that Booth wanted to see me. I went to the curb and met him. Booth apologized to me for the words he had used at the meeting, remarking that he thought that I must have been drunk in making the objections that I did in reference to his proposed plan of carrying out the abduction. I told him no --- drunkenness was on his and his party's part; that I was never more sober in my life, and that what I said the night before I meant, and that the week would end my connection with the affair.

Another Plan Hatched.

"On March 17, 1865, about 2 o'clock, Booth and Herold met O'Laughlin and myself. Booth stated that he was told that the President was going to attend a theatrical performance out on Seventh street, at a soldiers' encampment or hospital at the outer edge of the city. Booth had previously sent a small, black box containing two carbines, a monkey wrench, ammunition and four pieces of rope by the porter of the National Hotel to our room at Mrs. Van Tyne's. Not wishing it to remain in our room, O'Laughlin sent the box to an acquaintance of his in Washington. This box was sent to our room in the early part of March, 1865, I think, and was removed in about a week or 10 days.

"After Booth and Herold met O'Laughlin and myself and made arrangements to go out to the performance on Seventh street, Booth, Herold and O'Laughlin went for the box containing the two carbines, etc. The understanding was that Herold was to take the box with Booth's horse and buggy to either

Surrattsville or T.B., and there meet us, in case the abduction was successful. This was the last time I saw Herold until our trial.

"O'Laughlin returned and we took our dinner at the Franklin Hotel, as usual. After dinner we met Booth and accompanied him to the livery stable near the Patent Office, at which place Booth obtained horses for us. O'Laughlin and I then rode to our room on D street and made all our necessary arrangements, each arming himself. O'Laughlin and I then rode out to where the performance was to take place.

"We stopped at a restaurant at the foot of the hill to await the arrival of the other parties. They not arriving as soon as we expected, we remounted our horses and rode out the road about a mile. We then returned and stopped at the same restaurant. Whilst in there Atzerodt came in, having just arrived with Payne. A short time after Booth and Surratt came in and we drank together. Booth had made inquiries at the encampment where the performance was to be held, and learned that the president was not there. After telling us this we separated, O'Laughlin and myself riding back to the city together. Surratt and Booth rode out the road towards the country. O'Laughlin and I left our horses back of the National Hotel, at a livery stable.

Conspiracy Abandoned.

"About 8 o'clock I met Booth and Surratt near the stable. This was the last time I ever saw Surratt, and I never saw Payne after we parted in our ride into the city until the day of our trial. O'Laughlin and I left Washington on March 20 and went to Baltimore. Booth went to New York, and thus I thought the whole affair abandoned. I then told my family I had ceased business in Washington and had severed my connection with Booth.

"My father told me that if I would apply to J.W. Wharton for employment I might obtain it, as Wharton was looking for a clerk the last time he came up from Old Point Comfort, Va. to Baltimore. I went to my brother's home at Hookstown, Baltimore county, and I returned March 25 to Baltimore. I was informed at my father's that Booth had called to see me, and left a card requesting me to call upon him at Barnum's Hotel. I found a letter there, also, from him for me, in which he stated he desired to give it another trial the week following, and, if unsuccessful, to abandon it forever. The letter found in Booth's trunk was in answer to this letter, which I innocently wrote to prevent his undertaking it.

"On the same day --- March 27, 1865 --- I applied to J.W. Wharton, at Old Point Comfort, for employment and received a favorable answer to my application on March 31, 1865. O'Laughlin came to my father's, to which place I had returned from my brother's, and requested me to accompany him to Washington to see Booth, for the purpose of obtaining $500, which Booth had borrowed from him. I went with him that morning and returned with him in the early afternoon train of the same day. At the depot at Washington we accidentally met Atzerodt. We drank together and then parted from him. I never saw him from the 17th of March until then, and never afterward until our trial.

Surratt in Richmond.

"We saw Booth. During our conversation he told us that the president was not in Washington. He also said that Surratt had gone to Richmond, as he had understood through Weichman that a Mrs. Slator had arrived from Canada with dispatches, and that the party who had been in the habit of ferrying persons across the river had been arrested by the government, in consequence of which Surratt offered his services to accompany her to Richmond. I asked if he had received my letter of the 27th, and he replied that he had not. I asked him when the letter was received to destroy it. He told me he would.

"This interview on March 31 took place in his room at the National Hotel, Booth, O'Laughlin and myself being present. In this conversation Booth stated that the enterprise was abandoned. He also stated that he intended to return to his profession. It was at this interview that I asked Booth what I should do with the arms I had. He told me to keep them, to sell them, or do anything I desired with them. We left him at his room at the hotel about 2 o'clock in the afternoon, and after that time I never received either a letter from him or any other communication, nor he from me; neither have I seen him since.

NOTES

Notes to Introduction

1. These bits of information are contained in Record Group 153, Investigation and Trial Papers Relating to Suspects in the Lincoln Assassination. These papers are reproduced for greater accessibility in Microcopy M-599 (16 reels) by the National Archives. In this work, the source will be referred to as the Lincoln Assassination Suspects File (LAS), followed by the Reel and frame number at which the document appears. Regarding Atzerodt, see LAS, Reel III, frame 557; Herold, Reel IV, frame 402; O'Laughlen, Reel III, frame 611.

2. For John Broom, see LAS, Reel III, frame 495; Robert Mowry, Reel III, frame 507. For the "sketch" of Arnold, see Reel III, frame 611.

3. Pitman, Benn (ed.) *The Assassination of President Lincoln and the Trial of the Conspirators* (Cincinnati: Moore, Wilstach & Baldwin, 1865) was the official version of the trial testimony. For testimony of William Arnold, Frank Arnold, and Jacob Smith, see p. 240; for that of Charles Hall, George Craig, Minnie Poole, and John Wharton, see p. 241.

4. Ford's comments were published in the *Baltimore Gazette*, June 16, 1878, p. 1.

5. For the end of Surratt's lecture tour, see the *Richmond Daily Enquirer*, January 3, 1871, p.3, c.1. My thanks to Betty J. Ownsbey for this information.

Notes to Chapter One

1. The relative has not been identified, and the original letter has disappeared -- perhaps during the fire of February, 1904, which destroyed most of downtown Baltimore, including the offices of the *American*. In response to a correspondent in 1906, Arnold said he believed the newspaper's files, including photographs of himself, were lost in the fire. This second letter is now in a private collection.

2. Arnold refers to the reward claim of detective Eaton Horner, which was rejected by the War Department in 1866. Mr. Maulsby is Philip H. Maulsby, a brother-in-law of Michael O'Laughlen. The five words spoken by Arnold at his arrest were not reported at all.

3. This committee, headed by Benjamin F. Butler, of Massachusetts, tried to implicate President Andrew Johnson in the assassination.

4. "Death Recalls Great Tragedy," *Baltimore American*, October 9, 1902, p. 13. Arnold's reclusive lifestyle had led many to overlook him completely, and it was often assumed that he had passed away. See, for example, "John H. Surratt, Sole Survivor of Those Accused of Plotting," *The Springfield* (Mass.) *Daily Republican*, October 21, 1901.

5. Surratt lived out his years at 1016 W. Lanvale St., Baltimore.

6. For a fuller discussion of Mary Surratt, see Guy W. Moore, *The Case of Mary Surratt* (Norman, Okla.: University of Oklahoma Press, 1953).

7. "Payne" was an alias of Lewis Thornton Powell, a young Florida soldier and the strongman of the Booth conspiracy.

8. Edman Spangler received a sentence of six years, not life. Michael O'Laughlen died in prison.

9. This diary has not been located.

10. Arnold's source was *The Assassination of President Lincoln and the Trial of the Conspirators* (Cincinnati: Moore, Wilstach and Baldwin, 1865) 236, edited by Benn Pitman. The original letter is in the LAS File, Reel XV, frame 343.

Notes to Chapter Two

1. "Our American Cousin" was a popular English comedy, written by Tom Taylor and brought to America in the late 1850's by Laura Keene. On the night of the assassination, Miss Keene was marking her 1000th performance in the role of Florence Trenchard.

2. The man who grappled with Booth was Henry Reed Rathbone, 27, who reported hearing the assassin say the word "Freedom" just after firing the shot. Pitman, p. 78. While eyewitness accounts differ, this version of the shooting is typical of those published in 1865. Recent study suggests Booth actually broke his leg when his horse stumbled during the escape, and not

on the stage at Ford's. See Michael W. Kauffman, "Booth's Escape Route: Lincoln's Assassin On The Run," *Blue and Gray*, June, 1990, p. 17.

3. Clara Hamilton Harris was the fiancee of Major Rathbone. She was a daughter of New York Senator Ira Harris.

4. The Confederate conspiracy theory was recently revived, with newly discovered evidence, by William A. Tidwell, James O. Hall, and David Winfred Gaddy in *Come Retrubution: The Confederate Secret Service and the Assassination of Lincoln* (Jackson, Miss: University Press of Mississippi, 1988).

5. Joseph H. Barrett, *Life of Abraham Lincoln* (Cincinnati: Moore, Wilstach & Baldwin, 1865). The quoted passage begins on p. 798.

6. Eventually, most of those named in Johnson's proclamation were captured, but none ever faced trial. The reward money was ultimately paid for the capture of Davis.

Notes to Chapter Three

1. Louis J. Weichmann wrote his own account of the conspiracy and trial. Edited by Floyd E. Risvold, the Weichmann manuscript was published in 1975 under the title *A True History of the Assassination of Abraham Lincoln and of the Conspiracy of 1865* (New York: Alfred A. Knopf).

2. Brevet Major General John F. Hartranft

3. The trial and execution were held at the old penitentiary, just north of the Washington Arsenal in the southwest part of the city. In 1862, all prisoners had been transferred to Albany, N.Y., and the old penitentiary building was absorbed into the Arsenal complex. The former cellblock was used primarily for storage until the Lincoln conspiracy trial was held there in 1865. The Arsenal and penitentiary have since become Fort Lesley J. McNair. Michael W. Kauffman, "Fort Lesley J. McNair and the Lincoln Conspirators," *Lincoln Herald* 80 (Winter 1978).

4. Gen. Winfield Scott Hancock, then commander of the XXII Army Corps, which included all defenses of Washington

5. On June 17, 1869, Anna married William P. Tonry, who was then promptly fired from his position as a chemist in the government.

6. Hancock won the 1880 Democratic nomination in short order, handily defeating eighteen other candidates on the second ballot. Judging by his private correspondence, he did not seem to regard the Surratt issue as a serious threat to his political career. Winfield S. Hancock Papers, Military Academy Library, West Point.

7. King committed suicide by jumping into the Hudson River on November 13, 1865; James H. Lane shot himself on July 11, 1866 at Fort Leavenworth, Kansas.

Notes to Chapter Four

1. The original notarized statement can be found in the Benjamin F. Butler Papers, Manuscript Division, Library of Congress, Container 175. Arnold's misspellings were corrected in the published version.

2. Booth invested $6,000 in Pennsylvania oil stock, but never lived to see a profit. However, his shares in the Dramatic Oil Company eventually paid dividends to his brother, Junius, and his sister, Rosalie. Theatre manager John T. Ford estimated Booth's income from acting at about $20,000 per year, but Booth gave up his profession in 1864 to devote all his time to the conspiracy. See Ernest C. Miller, *John Wilkes Booth in the Pennsylvania Oil Region* (Meadville, Pa.: Crawford County Historical Society, 1987).

3. Booth returned from Canada at the end of October, and visited Southern Maryland in mid-November.

4. Rullman's was commonly known as the Lichau House.

5. Samuel Knapp Chester, an actor and close friend of Booth, refused to join the conspiracy despite Booth's intense efforts to recruit him. Chester's detailed statement is in LAS, beginning at Reel IV, frame 141. See also his testimony in Pitman, p. 44.

6. Mary Ann Booth was troubled by her occasional dreams about John Wilkes, and in this particular instance, her forebodings appear to have paid off. The 1865 diary of Junius Brutus Booth (Mugar Library, Boston University) confirms that Junius went to see John in early February, 1865. On February 10, President Lincoln and General Grant attended a play together at Ford's Theatre. Booth, however, was out of town, having left Washington shortly after talking with his brother. Arnold was apparently never aware that Booth had missed a chance to abduct the president. For

more on Mary Ann Booth's dreams, see Asia Booth Clarke, *The Unlocked Book* (New York: G.P. Putnam's Sons, 1938) p. 41. Lincoln's theatre appearance was mentioned in *The Washington Star*, February 11, 1865, p. 2.

7. Gautier's was located off Pennsylvania Avenue, between 11th and 12th Streets, Northwest.

8. Lincoln was expected to attend "Still Waters Run Deep" at the Campbell Hospital, on Seventh Street.

9. John Surratt's version of this incident is somewhat more specific. Surratt claimed the president had sent Chief Justice Salmon P. Chase in his place, but Chase's diaries cast doubt on the story. Lincoln himself was at the National Hotel, speaking to the 140th Indiana Regiment. For Surratt's account, see *The New York Times*, February 7, 1909, Pt. V, p. 3.

10. Sarah Antoinette Slater was the lady spy; the man was Augustus Spencer Howell, who had been arrested March 24th in the Surratt Tavern. See James O. Hall, "The Lady in the Veil" *Maryland Independent*, June 25, 1975, p. 1. See also testimony of David Barry in *The Trial of John Surratt* (Washington: Government Printing Office, 1867) p. 751. Howell's original statement is in the John T. Ford Papers, Manuscript Division, Maryland Historical Society, MS 371.

Notes to Chapter Five

1. The original statement is in the Benjamin F. Butler Papers, Library of Congress. In the same file is Gleason's own affidavit describing the circumstances under which Arnold's questioning took place. Gleason said of Arnold: "He seemed to be very careful and anxious to give a complete and full statement and I have no doubt of its truth and think it should receive full credence."

2. Captain Edward R. Dorsey commanded Company C, whose original roster can be found in the Manuscripts Division, Maryland Historical Society, MS 1239. Sam Arnold's brother Charles was a corporal in this company.

3. Capt. George Arnold, C.S.A., worked in the Nitre and Mining Bureau at Augusta.

4. The younger brother was Charles Albert Arnold (b. March 28, 1840).

5. Mary Jane Bland Arnold continued to deteriorate from her condition; she passed away November 13, 1865. Records of Green Mount Cemetery, Baltimore.

6. Arnold's father lived near the corner of Park Avenue and Fayette Street in downtown Baltimore. His brother, William Stockton Arnold (b. March 6, 1845) lived near Pimlico in a small house that stood at the southeast corner of Trainor and Park Heights Avenues. The name Hookstown has not been used locally since about 1870, when the neighborhood became Arlington. See Percy E. Martin, "Sam Arnold and Hookstown." *History Trails* 16 (Summer 1982), pp. 13-16.

7. Booth's last tour as an actor ended April 3, 1864 at the St. Charles Theatre in New Orleans.

8. In January, 1865, John Surratt and Thomas H. Harbin purchased two boats from Richard M. Smoot and J. Alexander Brawner of Charles County, Md. Richard Mitchell Smoot, *The Unwritten History of the Assassination of Abraham Lincoln* (Clinton, Mass.: W.J. Coulter, 1908) p. 8.

9. Henry E. Purdy, George Grillet, and John R. Giles testified at the conspiracy trial. Very likely, Daniel Loughran was one of the other men whose names Arnold forgot. See Pitman, pp. 230-231.

10. Weichmann was an employe of the Commissary General of Prisoners.

Notes to Chapter Six

1. The original manuscript says thirty-five years. Arnold was released in 1869, and his manuscript was published thirty-three years later.

2. The military commission to which Arnold refers consisted of nine officers selected by Gen. Edward D. Townsend and appointed by President Johnson. Their proceedings were published verbatim in various newspapers and in two carelessly compiled book versions of the testimony: *The Trial of the Assassins and Conspirators* (Philadelphia: T.B. Peterson & Brothers, 1865) and *The Conspiracy Trial for the Murder of The President*, edited by Ben: Perley Poore (Boston: J.E. Tilton and Company, 1865, 3 vols.). A third version was paraphrased, indexed, and published with the War Department's sanction: *The Assassination of President Lincoln and the Trial of the Conspirators*, edited by Benn Pitman (Cincinnati: Moore, Wilstach & Baldwin, 1865). The last of these, hereinafter cited as Pitman, is the most easily accessible. All were reprinted in subsequent editions.

3. Born September 6, 1834

4. The date of this meeting cannot be fixed with certainty, but it can be estimated at around August 8th. Arnold places this meeting before Booth became ill somewhere up north. According to notes kept by Junius Booth, Jr., John Wilkes and his brother Edwin went from New York to Philadelphia together on August 2nd, and John left the latter city on the 7th, heading for Washington. Most likely, Booth stopped in Baltimore on this trip; he doesn't seem to have had another chance. Beginning on about August 11th, Booth suffered from erysipelas in his right elbow -- the illness to which Arnold referred -- and for the next three weeks was laid up in bed at his sister's house in Philadelphia. After this, Booth went to the oil region in western Pennsylvania to settle his affairs. Junius Booth diary for 1864, Folger Shakespeare Library, Washington.

5. William S. Arnold was the messenger. "Willie" attended St. Timothy's Hall with his brother. He may have seen Booth on a visit to the Holliday Street Theatre in Baltimore. According to John T. Ford (who owned the Holliday as well as Ford's Theatre in Washington), Willie was in the habit of hanging around the Baltimore theatre, and Booth stopped by whenever he was in the area. See Ford's statement to Col. Henry S. Olcott, dated April 28, 1865. LAS, Reel V, frame 441.

6. Prisoners of war had been exchanged since a cartel arrangement had been worked out in 1862. General Grant, however, felt the South benefitted more from the policy than did the North. In early 1864, he had recommended the exchange be stopped, and Lincoln agreed. Southerners charged that this was cruel to the prisoners, as the Confederacy no longer had the means to feed and care for their captives. Without an exchange or a wholesale release, they said, these men would die of starvation. By August, deaths were occurring in large numbers, and great pressure fell upon the administration to resume the exchange in the name of humanity. Thus the prisoner exchange issue gave a strong humanitarian appeal to Booth's recruiting for the conspiracy.

7. Arnold's original manuscript mentions some of the conspirators' activities in the early fall of 1864. They planned to meet again when Booth returned from a trip North to settle his affairs, but this meeting was delayed by Booth's illness. In late October, Booth went to Canada in order to ship his wardrobe from Montreal to the Confederate States by way of Nassau, Bahamas. He returned in November with a letter of introduction to Dr. William Queen, of Charles County, Maryland. In November and December, Booth travelled extensively in Southern Maryland, trying to learn the roads and river crossings. As a cover story, he claimed to be

looking for real estate to buy in the area.

Arnold briefly mentions the letter of introduction, but gives no details. The letter was given to Booth by Patrick C. Martin, a Baltimorean and a Confederate official living in Montreal at the time. This letter did much to facilitate Booth's eventual escape from Washington, as it brought the actor into the underground network of operatives who routinely transported people and mail across enemy lines.

8. This meeting took place at the National Hotel in January, when Arnold and Surratt happened to visit Booth at the same time. See Arnold's notarized statement of 1867.

9. The dates of these occurrences are unknown.

10. Arnold was unaware that Booth traveled to New York during this period with Lewis T. Powell. George A. Atzerodt statement, May 1, 1865, published in the *Surratt Courier*, October, 1988, p. 1. (The original statement is now in a private collection.) Also LAS, Reel VI, frame 499. John H. Surratt visited Booth in New York during this period as well. He was introduced there to Booth's mother, and to his brother, Edwin. Louis J. Weichmann testimony in *Trial of John Surratt*, p. 375. En route to New York, Booth stopped at the home of his sister, Asia Booth Clarke, in Philadelphia.

11. Confederate soldiers raided the town of St. Albans, Vermont, along the Canadian border, on October 17, 1864. See Jon Woodward "The St. Albans Raid: Rebels in Vermont," *Blue and Gray*, 8 (December, 1990) p. 9.

12. Booth had helped Chester, an actor and lifelong friend, get his job in the stock company of the Winter Garden Theatre, New York, which was then under the management of Edwin Booth and John Sleeper Clarke. To further his conspiracy, John Wilkes Booth tried to secure a job for Chester at Ford's Theatre in Washington. Chester, though, reacted with horror when Booth laid out his proposal. His detailed statement to authorities is in LAS, Reel IV, frame 141. See also his testimony at the Conspiracy Trial. Pitman, p. 44.

Notes to Chapter Seven

1. Booth normally stayed at the National Hotel, on Pennsylvania Avenue at Sixth Street. According to the hotel's clerk, George W. Bunker, Booth checked out on January 28th and did not return until February 22nd. See Bunker testimony in Pitman, p. 46.

2. The original manuscript says "inauguration," and this occasion (March 4, 1865) is undoubtedly what Arnold had in mind.

3. Michael O'Laughlen was said to have told his captors that he, too, had abandoned the scheme after the prisoner exchange had been reinstated. The date that he became aware of of the administration's policy change is not easy to determine; newspaper reports indicated a piecemeal resumption of the old arrangement, and many exceptions were made for special cases. Large scale exchanges had come about by January, 1865. For O'Laughlen comments, see *The New York Herald*, April 19, 1865, p. 1.

4. The next sentence omitted here in the *American* was an important one: "Association he deemed bound us irrevocably to him from which we could not wrench ourselves." John Wilkes Booth had already told a number of people that it would do no good to betray him, as their association had already established the guilt of all who knew about the plot. In this way, Booth was able to guarantee the silence, if not the loyalty, of those who were aware of the conspiracy. For example, see the statement of Samuel K. Chester, LAS, Reel IV, frame 141.

5. Arnold makes it plain that the stockade was being built at the Benning Bridge. On the night of the assassination, Booth used the Navy Yard Bridge instead. Both were heavily guarded, but the glib and persuasive Booth was able to talk his way past the guard. Despite sensationalist claims to the contrary, the Navy Yard Bridge sentry had been given strict orders not to allow anyone to pass on the night of the assassination. See records of the XXII Army Corps, National Archives.

6. The meeting adjourned at 5 a.m. on March 16th.

7. Booth allegedly owed O'Laughlen $500, which he promised to repay when he returned from New York. Arnold agreed to accompany O'Laughlen to Washington on March 31st to ask for the money. Memo of Police Marshal Thomas Carmichael. LAS, Reel IV, frame 197.

8. Louis J. Weichmann's job at the office of the Commissary General of Prisoners gave him access to privileged information, but he claimed to have passed only those figures that had become public knowledge by their appearance in the newspapers. The woman mentioned here was Sarah A. Slater, and the man who had been arrested was Augustus Spencer Howell, mentioned above. Louis J. Weichmann letter to Henry L. Burnett, May 28, 1865. LAS, Reel III, frame 105.

9. Sketchy or incorrect accounts of the assassination were not uncommon, and many wild rumors made their way into the news reports. On April 20th, a Sanitary Commission employe at Fortress Monroe wrote of Arnold: "he is said to have confessed that he had taken for his share [in the plot] the destruction of the Fortress by blowing up two of the more accessible of its magazines....Arnold is said to have tampered with some of the garrison in order to get an opportunity to carry out his plans." Edward Williams Morley Papers, Manuscripts Division, Library of Congress.

10. This is not a correct transcription of Arnold's manuscript, and he called the matter to the editor's attention shortly after the series was published. See the correction, p.179

11. Arnold took exception to the testimony of Eaton G. Horner, as paraphrased in the official trial account: "At first [Arnold] denied, but on my mentioning the letter that had been found in Booth's trunk, mailed at Huntstown [*sic*], he admitted that he wrote that letter." Pitman, p. 235.

12. The detectives had evidently misled Arnold, and he never learned of the deception. O'Laughlen was arrested on Monday -- too late for the detectives to have known about his surrender to Detective William E. Wallis. The men who took Arnold into custody had only gone to Fortress Monroe after failing to locate O'Laughlen in Baltimore. See the Thomas Carmichael memo. LAS, Reel IV, frame 197; Undated William McPhail letter. LAS, Reel II, frame 986; and Carmichael's memo to McPhail, dated July 14, 1865. Records of the Adjutant General's Office, M-619, Reel 458, frame 263. Arnold's complete original statement is published in Appendix A.

13. The only property mentioned in official correspondence consisted of a black travelling bag with a pistol, serial number 164557; a small tin can of cartridges; a batch of private letters; and $27.50 in cash. Henry L. Burnett letter to Col. Timothy Ingraham, dated May 18, 1865. LAS, Reel I, frame 42; and M-619, Reel 458, frame 326. A Bowie knife and another pistol, serial number 117808, was found in a search of Willie Arnold's house at Hookstown. M-619, Reel 458, frame 324. On July 31, 1865, Gen. Hartranft sent Capt. Richard A. Watts to deliver the $27.50 to George W. Arnold in Baltimore. The signed receipt is in the Hartranft Papers, Gettysburg College.

14. Col. John W. Woolley, of Indiana, was the provost marshal on the staff of Maj. Gen. Lew Wallace, based in Baltimore. Wallace, who served on the commission that tried Arnold, later became famous as the author of *Ben Hur*.

15. Lewis Powell had attempted to dash out his brains on the bulkhead of the *Montauk*. This led to the issuing of the order of April 23rd, which called for the canvas hoods "to prevent self-destruction". David M. DeWitt, *The Judicial Murder of Mary E. Surratt* (Baltimore: John Murphy & Co., 1895) p. 13. A similar order emanating from Stanton's office was the one issued April 29, 1865 to Gen. Winfield S. Hancock, commanding the Middle Military Division, to provide for the "secure detention" of the prisoners, with emphasis on preventing their self-destruction. Stanton Papers, Reel 9, Manuscript Division, Library of Congress.

16. The ship was the U.S.S. *Saugus*, lying at anchor off the Navy Yard along with the *Montauk*. The ship's log recorded Arnold's arrival at 2:00 on April 19th. Arnold's wrist restraints were of a type called "Lilly irons," after their inventor, Sgt. Robert Lilly, U.S. Marine Corps. The actual irons used in this case are on display in the Lincoln Museum at Ford's Theatre. They are on loan from the Smithsonian Institution.

17. Captain Frank Munroe, U.S. Marine Corps

Notes to Chapter Eight

1. The order was issued April 23rd. Dewitt, p. 13.

2. The order for Arnold's transfer specified that it should take place as soon after 8 p.m. as the prison cells were ready. Edwin M. Stanton to Winfield S. Hancock, April 29, 1865 in Stanton Papers, Reel 9, Library of Congress.

3. Arnold was correct. He was aboard the *Keyport*, a side-wheeled vessel being leased to the government.

4. Initially, all prisoners were placed in cells on the first of four tiers in the cellblock. Mrs. Surratt and some of those who were not on trial were soon moved to the second tier. Throughout the trial, Arnold remained in cell 184. Hartranft Papers, Gettysburg College.

5. During their incarceration at the penitentiary, prisoners were fed at 8 a.m., noon (or during the court's recess) and 5 p.m. daily. Meals consisted of a piece of cold salt pork or beef, one slice of soft bread, and water. For the evening meal, coffee was substituted for the water. Mrs. Surratt did not share in this diet; she generally took *t*oast and tea. Herold's sisters often brought him soda crackers and strawberries. Hartranft papers.

6. Fort Washington, Maryland lies on the Potomac River opposite Mt. Vernon.

7. Congressman John A. Bingham, Republican of Ohio.

8. The hoods were said to have been made by Priscilla Dodd, wife of the general. They are now owned by the Smithsonian Institution, and replicas of them are on display in the Lincoln Museum at Ford's Theatre.

9. Mrs. Surratt and Dr. Mudd were apparently not hooded, though Mudd was heavily ironed like the other men. Dr. George Loring Porter, assistant surgeon, recommended the hoods be removed, and that the prisoners be allowed to have exercise and reading material. His report on the matter was prompted by Edman Spangler's apparent mental "wandering", first noticed on June 17th. Hartranft Papers; George L. Porter, "How Booth's Body Was Hidden," *Columbian Magazine*, April, 1911, p. 74.

10. Four detectives were assigned to duty at the penitentiary, but were specifically forbidden to speak to any of the prisoners. Edwin M. Stanton to Winfield S. Hancock, April 29, 1865, Stanton Papers, Reel 9. Atzerodt did have at least one visit from Marshal McPhail, however. This occurred on May 10th. Hartranft Papers. Of all the defendants, Atzerodt seemed most eager to talk.

11. The Hartranft Papers show this as June 18th, but Edman Spangler also remembered the date as the 10th. Spangler account in John T. Ford Papers, Maryland Historical Society, MS 371.

12. Surratt claimed to have been at Elmira, New York at the time of the assassination. He was looking over the prisoner of war camp there in anticipation of a possible prisoner rescue mission.

13. This policy did not apply to all prisoners. On May 17th, Gen. Hancock granted permission for an unnamed inmate to have a prayer book. This might have been Willie Jett, a witness being kept in custody, who had requested one earlier. Hartranft Papers.

14. On July 7, 1865 four prisoners were executed in the prison yard. They were Mary E. Surratt, Lewis Powell, David Herold, and George Atzerodt.

15. Dr. Samuel Mudd, Michael O'Laughlen, and Samuel Arnold were sentenced to life in prison. Edman Spangler was sentenced to six years in prison, and all terms were to be served at the penitentiary at Albany, N.Y. On July 15th, President Johnson secretly modified the sentences, and sent

all four to the Dry Tortugas instead of Albany.

16. Captain William Budd, U.S. Navy

17. Capt. George W. Dutton, 10th Veteran Reserve Corps

18. Edman Spangler recalled that the leg irons cut his ankles right to the bone. Spangler statement, Ford Papers, Maryland Historical Society.

Notes to Chapter Nine

1. Though construction began on the fort in the 1840's, it was not fully garrisoned until January, 1861. Fort Jefferson operated under the command of the Department of the Gulf, and remained an active post until the Army abandoned it in January, 1874. It was transferred to the Engineer Corps on June 27, 1884, and was unoccupied until the Spanish-American War, May–July, 1898. Two years later, the fort was transferred to the Navy Department to serve as a refueling station. In 1908 the Navy relinquished its title to the Department of Agriculture. Since the 1930s it has been owned by the National Park Service, and is now a National Monument and part of the Everglades Park. It is accessible through privately operated boat and seaplane services.

2. The actual number of prisoners on the fort decreased dramatically during the period of Arnold's incarceration. On March 1, 1866 there were 207 inmates serving time there; when Arnold was released three years later, only 36 prisoners remained. Many prisoners arrived at the fort in poor health, or were "being daily taken sick with disease incidental to the climate," according to the prison staff. Records of Continental Commands, Fort Jefferson Morning Reports for 1866, and Lt. Frank Thorp to Bvt. Lt.Col. E.C. Bainbridge, June 3, 1868 in Letters Sent by the Provost Marshal. Record Group 393, Part V, National Archives.

3. Mudd tried to stow away on the transport *Thomas A. Scott*, but was discovered in a few minutes. As the prisoner explained to his attorney, he tried to escape because he had been led to believe that "our former privileges would be denied & that life would be very insecure." Mudd letter to Thomas Ewing, Jr., dated October 22, 1865, in Ewing Family Papers, Library of Congress. The escape attempt, and its consequences, are described more fully in Nettie Mudd, *The Life of Dr. Samuel A. Mudd* (New York and Washington: The Neale Publishing Company, 1906) p. 120-127. A fanciful woodcut of Mudd's attempt was published in *Harper's Weekly*, October 21, 1865, based on a drawing made by a passenger on the ship. It shows Lt. Arthur Tappan, lantern in hand, discovering Mudd's feet

sticking out of a cannon barrel. In reality, Mudd hid below decks. On August 20th, several prisoners had made their escape in the same way, but Mudd was quite famous, and was recognized at once.

4. Grenfell, a British-born soldier of fortune, had been imprisoned for the so-called Northwest Conspiracy to release prisoners of war from Camp Douglas in Chicago. Born May 30, 1808, the colonel was 57 years old. Stephen Z. Starr, *Colonel Grenfell's Wars* (Baton Rouge: Louisiana State University Press, 1971) p. 17.

5. On September 16, 1865, Lt. George S. Carpenter reported to Adjutant General Edward D. Townsend on conditions at Fort Jefferson. Carpenter (whom Arnold mentions later) had visited the fort in response to General Baker's warning of a rescue plot. His report mentioned numerous breaches of security and at least one recent (August 20th) attempt to escape aboard the steamer *Thomas A. Scott*. This September 16th report recommended leg irons and "strict surveillance" for the "state prisoners." It is undoubtedly the source of their grave discomfort, and its timing --- just before Mudd's escape attempt --- is coincidental. Fort Jefferson miscellaneous files, Record Group 393, National Archives.

6. Lafayette Curry Baker had been the chief of the National Detective Police, which was loosely styled the Secret Service, but not the forerunner of that federal agency. Baker was a highly controversial official who was said to be unscrupulous in the extreme. The addressee of this memorandum was Gen. Thomas T. Eckert, former head of the War Department Telegraph Office.

7. Mudd was forced to wheel sand from one place to another. At one point he was given the task of cleaning old bricks; he wrote his wife that it was hard work, and he could almost manage to finish one brick in a single day. Prison records show that he served much of his sentence in the fort's carpentry shop, and as a clerk in the office of the provost marshal. Mudd, p. 124 and Fort Jefferson miscellaneous records, Record Group 393, National Archives.

8. Gen. John G. Foster

9. Gen. John Newton, commander of the District of Middle Florida

Notes to Chapter Ten

1. This document and related material can be found in the reports of Generals John Newton and James Forsyth relative to charges of mistreatment of prisoners at Fort Jefferson. File 507 N 1865, Records of the Adjutant General's Office, Record Group 94, National Archives. Published on microfilm as Microcopy M-619, Reel 391, beginning at frame 258.

2. The provost marshal was 2nd Lt. Joseph Keeffe, Fifth U.S. Artillery, mentioned above.

3. 1st Lt. William Van Reed, mentioned above

4. Arnold's manuscript identifies the man responsible for the prisoners' transfer as Brevet Major Benjamin F. Rittenhouse, Fifth U.S. Artillery. Rittenhouse commanded the prison bakery, but served occasionally as the fort's adjutant or provost marshal.

5. Despite the hardships and cruel treatment, all of the so-called conspirators were allowed to correspond with whomever they chose, apparently without censorship. Dr. Mudd complained often to his wife, Sarah Frances Mudd, and in this case his complaints paid off. For Mudd's prison correspondence, see Nettie Mudd, *The Life of Dr. Samuel A. Mudd*. A recent edition, still available, was issued by Dr. Richard D. Mudd (Linden, Tenn.: The Continental Book Company, 1975).

6. Grenfell arrived at Fort Jefferson on October 8, 1865, having passed through Fort Wood, N.Y. He had been transferred from the state penitentiary at Columbus, Ohio to the Dry Tortugas, and he began the journey on September 19th. Starr, p. 274.

Notes to Chapter Eleven

1. Thompson P. McElrath, of New York City, owned the diary until his death in 1898. Stephen Starr tried, without success, to trace its whereabouts in 1971. McElrath published excerpts of the diary in "Annals of the War...Story of a Soldier of Fortune." *Philadelphia Weekly Times*, May 3, 1879.

2. Many charges of cruelty were investigated in 1866. The resulting documentation is accessible in File 830 A 1866 in the Papers of the Advocate General's Office, Record Group 94, National Archives. This has been published on microfilm as Microcopy M-619, Reel 451, beginning at frame 439.

3. Arnold identified this sergeant as 1st Sgt. John Murphy, Co. I, Fifth U.S. Artillery. Murphy, a career soldier, was commissioned a second lieutenant on August 16, 1867. He retired as a Major and paymaster in 1899, and was promoted to the rank of lieutenant colonel on the retired list five years later. Military Pension file, National Archives.

4. "Stebb" in the original; the man was Private Andrew Steb, Company I, Fifth U.S. Artillery. Steb told investigators that he was accidentally pushed and sustained a scratch on his face. His full statement is in Record Group 94, National Archives. Microcopy M-619, Reel 451, frame 548.

5. Private Ernest Nickel, Co. F, Fifth U.S. Artillery, suffered a severe injury to his fingers. A statement by Corporal Robert C. Brown, a witness, termed this an accident. Privates Nickel and Steb (note 3, above) were both injured by Sgt. John Murphy.

6. The only soldier named Conrad listed on the company muster roll was Ferdinand Conrad. In the original manuscript, Brevet Major Benjamin F. Rittenhouse is identified as the abuser of Conrad.

7. Brevet Major John Bell, Assistant Surgeon, U.S. Army

8. Brevet Major Charles C. MacConnell, Co. C, Fifth U.S. Artillery, was officer of the day, and Sgt. Edward Donnelly, Co. L, was sergeant of the guard. According to Arnold, MacConnell was quite drunk when this incident occurred. On November 25, 1866, Major Wallace Randolph submitted a report on the incident to Colonel George L. Gillespie. Among other things, Randolph stated that Dunn was not badly mistreated, that he was currently engaged in playing the violin at the post theatre, and that Dunn wished to remain at the fort even after his sentence had been served. On the record, though, is Dunn's departure for New Orleans on November 28th, the day of his release. Secretary Stanton ordered that MacConnell and Maj. Rittenhouse both be court-martialed for mistreating prisoners. Randolph's report is in M-619, Reel 451, frame 550 and 578. The court martial order is on Reel 451, frame 483.

Notes to Chapter Twelve

1. Bradley T. Johnson, an attorney and former Confederate general from Maryland

2. The article first appeared in the New York *World*, November 1, 1866, p.5, and was reprinted in other newspapers throughout the country.

3. Grenfell actually kept a copy of the letter in his own handwriting. Telegram from Col. G.S. Gillespie to Gen. P.H. Sheridan in Microcopy M-619, Reel 451, frame 520, National Archives.

4. Pvt. Michael Gossner, of Buffalo, N.Y.

5. Pvt. Rensellear Durfee, of Washington, D.C.

6. General Hill's denial, dated November 29, 1866, is filed with Record Group 94, National Archives, Microcopy M-619, Reel 451, frame 446.

7. Brevet Lt. Col. George L. Gillespie, an engineer, led the investigation. His papers on the matter were designated as File 830 A 1866, and can be found in Record Group 94, cited above, beginning at frame 439.

8. 2nd Lt. M.C. Greer, Co. I, 5th U.S. Artillery, in "Rebel Slanders About Fort Jefferson," *Philadelphia Inquirer*, July 7, 1867, p. 1. Grier was not at Fort Jefferson when the atrocities were said to have occurred. Arnold might easily be justified in his assertion that the official report on the matter was whitewashed. During Col. Gillespie's investigation, some of the principal witnesses did not comment on the charges, while all those on record downplayed the severity of their treatment. The report itself cleared the officers of wrongdoing, but it was greeted with some cynicism in Washington. Secretary Stanton ordered that Maj. B.F. Rittenhouse and Capt. C.C. MacConnell be court-martialed for abusing prisoners. E.D. Townsend to B.H. Hill, November 24, 1866 in Record Group 94, Microcopy M-619, Reel 451, frame 483.

It should be noted that Arnold has already cited General Hill for an occasional act of kindness. From an examination of Hill's correspondence with the Grenfell family, it appears he was somewhat concerned for the welfare of his prisoner. See Starr, p. 284.

9. Major Benjamin F. Rittenhouse

10. Hill was replaced at the fort by Brevet Major Wallace R. Randolph, Fifth U.S. Artillery.

11. Dr. J. S. Holden was on duty at this time.

12. Robinson was the provost marshal.

Notes to Chapter Thirteen

1. The officers were 1st Lt. Frederick Robinson, 1st Lt. George W. Crabb, and 2nd Lt. Albert Pike, all of the Fifth U.S. Artillery.

2. In the original manuscript, Arnold mentions the presence of Provost Sgt. Michael Gleason and Acting Military Storekeeper George T. Jackson.

3. Lt. Robinson

4. Lt. Crabb

5. Pvt. John Fisher, of New York City

6. Perry Coffman, Co. L, Fifth U.S. Artillery

7. Sgt. Henry Schickhardt, Co. M

8. Pvt. (later Corporal) Charles R. Harris, Co. M, of New York City

9. Lt. Solon Orr

10. Major Andrews had served in California during the years 1862-65.

Notes to Chapter Fourteen

1. Capt. George W. Crabb evidently brought a mild case of the fever to Fort Jefferson when he returned from a trip to Cuba in August, 1867. Crabb recovered.

2. Mudd had been working in the prison dispensary when Dr. Smith became ill. Having encountered the disease before (during an outbreak in Baltimore twelve years before) Mudd was judged competent to take over in the crisis.

3. Yellow fever took its name from the jaundiced skin color of its victims. The disease typically began with chills, fever, severe abdominal pain, and vomiting. This would be followed by a brief lull in the symptoms. Sometimes the victim recovered at this point, but in many cases he would enter a final (usually fatal) stage: yellow skin; internal bleeding, marked by black vomit; and delirium.

4. The first case was recorded on August 19th, and the last on November 14th. Of about 400 people on the fort, 270 caught the disease, and of these 38 died. See Rodman Bethel, *A Slumbering Giant of the Past: Fort Jefferson, U.S.A. in the Dry Tortugas* (Hialeah, Fla.: W.L. Litho, 1979) pp.

47-48. Michael O'Laughlen and Pvt. James H. Markey were the only two prisoner fatalities. O'Laughlen showed the first symptoms on September 17th, and died on the 23rd. Dr. Mudd described his death thus: "O'Loughlin was taken day before yesterday, and was getting along very well up to late yesterday evening, when, owing to the imprudence of some visitor giving account of the recent deaths, he became excited, sank into a collapse....My heart almost fails me, but I must say he is dying....[later] O'Loughlin died this morning....We prolonged his suffering life for two days by constant nursing and attention." Mudd, pp. 265-267.

5. Dr. Daniel Whitehurst (1807-1872) was a former post surgeon at Fort Jefferson who had gone into private practice in Key West.

6. Dr. Edward Thomas

7. It is remarkable that nowhere in the manuscript does Arnold mention the death of his friend and cellmate, Mike O'Laughlen.

8. 2nd Lt. Edmund L. Zalinski

9. According to Dr. Mudd, Grenfell himself was severely suffering from the disease at this time. Mudd, p. 273.

10. William H. Gleason was from Biscayne Bay, Florida.

11. Gleason remained on the fort for two weeks. He recommended Arnold to Chairman Butler as a truthful witness, eager to answer all questions forthrightly. Gleason affidavit in Butler Papers, Library of Congress.

12. This was Brevet Maj. Charles C. MacConnell, who had been court-martialed as a result of Grenfell's expose. This woud happen to MacConnell again during the course of the coming year.

13. Lt. Frank Thorpe

Notes to Chapter Fifteen

1. Brevet Maj. Charles C. MacConnell's report to the Assistant Adjutant General in Key West was brief: Private William Noreil, Company I, deserted and took prisoners G. St. Leger Grenfell, J.W. Adare, James Orr and Joseph Holroyd with him. Grenfell had "considerable money in his possession by and through which he bribed the sentinel." MacConnell letter dated March 12, 1868 on P. 94, Regimental Letter Book of Fort Jefferson, Record Group 393, National Archives.

Prisoners were not allowed to keep more than $3 in their posses-
sion at any time. Unnumbered special order, dated October 20, 1865 in
Report 507 N 1865. Record Group 94, Microcopy M-619, Reel 391, frame
255, National Archives.

2. Dr. Mudd was pardoned first, as one of the final official acts of President
Andrew Johnson. Mudd received his pardon on March 8, 1869 and he left
the fort on March 11th.

3. Arnold's pardon, which was issued by President Johnson on March 1,
1869, came about after Maryland Governor Oden Bowie, along with the
mayor, police commissioner, city council, and judges of the city of
Baltimore, petitioned for his release. In all, more than 200 signatures
appeared on the request, including those of Marshal James L. McPlail and
numerous law enforcement officers.

In the course of his research for this account, Arnold requested a
copy of his pardon from the State Department. This copy, certified
September 11, 1894, is in the Maryland Historical Society, MS 1860. The
Pardon Attorney of the U.S. Justice Department kept a file on petitions for
Arnold's release. The file is designated B p.624, and it is located in Record
Group 204, National Archives.

4. Ewing was one of the nation's finest lawyers. A brother-in-law of
General William T. Sherman, he had been the first chief justice of the
Kansas Supreme Court. He and his father were partners to Lincoln's close
friend, Orville Hickman Browning, who had consulted on the petition for
Mary Surratt's *writ of habeas corpus*. Arnold's associate counsel in the
conspiracy trial was Walter Smith Cox, a capable young law professor who
would eventually preside over the trial of President Garfield's assassin,
Guiteau. Several collections of Ewing Papers exist, but most of the
attorneys' (father and son) correspondence relating to this case are in the
Ewing Family Papers, Manuscript Division, Library of Congress. This
collection has a wealth of material on Ewing's other client, Dr. Mudd, and
on the efforts to secure a pardon for Ned Spangler. The day The *American*
published its last article by Sam Arnold, General Ewing wrote to Arnold at
his home in Friendship, Md. Arnold's reply, dated December 23, 1902, is
in the Ewing Family Papers.

5. Ewing, like General Sherman, was an outspoken critic of the war
secretary.

6. The complete sentence, from the manuscript, is: "The less you say about
that the better; you have a d----d hard court to try you, and as for Judge
Holt, he is a G-d d----d murderer."

7. George W. Arnold visited his son in the courtroom on June 14th, and in the prison yard on July 9th, after the trial was over. Hartranft Letterbook, Hartranft Papers, pp. 64, 91.

Notes to Chapter Sixteen

1. Both Herold and Atzerodt tried repeatedly to write confessions in the mistaken belief that they could thus absolve themselves of all culpability in the assassination. Herold's attempts, made after hours in the courtroom, have not come to light. Hartranft Letterbook, p. 35. Gen. Ewing believed Herold's writings were in the possession of the Judge Advocate, and Ewing seemed to have an idea of their contents. Ewing to Andrew Johnson, July 12, 1865 in the Mudd Pardon File, Record Group 204, National Archives. Atzerodt's written confessions took at least two forms; one (now privately owned) was discovered in the 1970s among the papers of his attorney, and the other was given out to the press on several occasions. Neither was admissible in court, as argued by the defense attorneys themselves. See Pitman, p. 234. The recently discovered Atzerodt confession is published in the *Surratt Courier*, October, 1988, p. 1.

2. In the only confession he actually made to the War Department, Herold denied being in Washington on the night of the assassination. LAS, Reel IV, frame 441. Atzerodt's confession to Col. Henry H. Wells, given on May 2, 1865, described a meeting at the Herndon House in Washington, at 7 p.m. on the night of April 14th. LAS, Reel III, frame 596.

3. A number of witnesses were called to give this testimony in the early stages of the trial. Judge Advocate General Joseph Holt insisted on hearing their testimony in secret, but after several days Secretary of War Stanton overruled Holt and opened the trial for media coverage. Very shortly thereafter, the secret testimony was found to have been fraudulent, and the case against the Confederate government was dealt a serious blow.

4. Charles A. Dunham, who testified under the name of Sanford Conover, had brought seven witnesses to a Congressional committee in 1866 to offer testimony on the complicity of Confederate leaders. Two of the witnesses confessed that Dunham had written their stories for them, and that their testimony was false. Ultimately, all eight witnesses were discredited, and Conover was sentenced to ten years in prison for perjury. He was pardoned after serving a year. Conover/Dunham Pardon file B p. 576, in Record Group 204, National Archives.

5. The Spandauer story is mysterious. Benjamin Spandauer did not testify, though numerous articles claimed that he did. One such source also claimed (falsely) that Louis J. Weichmann, a prosecution witness, had died in Philadelphia in 1885. *The New York Times*, March 18, 1887, p. 1. Weichmann lived until 1902.

6. An exhaustive survey of witnesses is still underway, and incomplete at this writing. However, of the 200 witnesses traced thus far, only one (E.D.R. Bean) died before March of 1869. However, there is some validity to Arnold's charge that there were improprieties in the trial. Richard Roberts Montgomery's testimony had been taken in secret, and he could not be located for rebuttal. Several of the prosecution witnesses were convicted of fraud, perjury or other crimes, either before or after 1865. For example, Marcus P. Norton, a patent attorney who testified against Dr. Mudd, spent several years in the Massachusetts penitentiary for fraud in an unrelated case.

7. Judge Advocate General Holt died August 1, 1894. John A. Bingham died March 19, 1900 and Henry L. Burnett died January 4, 1916. Of nine members of the commission, five had died before Arnold's articles were published. They were: David R. Clendenin (d. March 5, 1895); James A. Ekin (d. March 27, 1891); Albion P. Howe (d. January 25, 1897); David Hunter (d. February 2, 1886); and August V. Kautz (d. September 4, 1895). Robert S. Foster died March 3, 1903, and the rest were still living at the time of Arnold's death: Thomas M. Harris (d. September 30, 1906 -- a week after Arnold); Lew Wallace (d. February 15, 1905); and Charles H. Tompkins (d. January 18, 1915).

8. Arnold lived on the farm of Anne Stockett Smith Garner, the mother of a close friend and schoolmate. The house still stands, largely unchanged through the years, on Fairhaven Road north of Friendship, Maryland.

Notes to Appendix A

1. Correspondence on this matter is located in the files of the Advocate General's Office, Record Group 94, Microcopy M-619, Reel 458, beginning at frame 240.

2. This undoubtedly refers to T.B., the village south of Surrattsville, where the guns were supposed to have been hidden.

Note to Appendix B

1. Robert Garner, like Arnold and Booth, attended St. Timothy's Hall in the early 1850's.

Notes to Appendix C

1. This is now 912 Montpelier Street.

2. Oreon Mann Arnold (b. November 12, 1853) was married to George Reingold Jackson, a Union veteran of the Civil War.

3. Michael O'Laughlen is also buried at Green Mount Cemetery.

Index